D1343831

Eyes on Africa

A Fifty Year Commentary

by
Ronald Watts

William Sessions Limited
York, England

ISBN 1 85072 327 3

Printed in 11 point Plantin Typeface
from Author's Disk
by Sessions of York
The Ebor Press
York, England

Contents

Photographs on Covers

ALL THE PHOTOGRAPHS on the front and back covers were taken by the author between 1965 and 2004. While his wife was i/c TB at Ngwelezane Hospital he became fascinated by the history of KwaZulu Natal. It is remarkable that the battlefields of the 1879 Anglo-Zulu War are being used to develop tourism and links with Wales. Many of the red coats who were slaughtered came from the barracks in Brecon.

On the top right the Queen is being welcomed by President Mugabe at Harare airport in 1991. Below tourists are arriving to visit the 'Roots' village on the River Gambia in 2004. The buffalo was wallowing in an Amboseli swamp in Kenya. The flowers are Protea's whose export from Zimbabwe was developed by a Quaker who moved from Harare to the Eastern Highlands. Below Dr. Watts's Tanzanian friend, Dr. Wilbert Chagula, posed in front of the newly built University of Dar-es-Salaam in 1965. On the right one of the author's students at Makerere University shows off his project.

On the back cover the first photo, taken in 1973 is of an Angolan woman working on a commercial farm south of Huambo. The second illustrates the contrast between a modest colonial building and a new skyscraper in 1990's Eldoret, Kenya. The elephant demonstrates how wildlife can live alongside people in the Zambezi Valley at Chirundu market. President Idi Amin visited the 1971 Open Day at the University Farm in Uganda and is shown watching a student's demonstration. Lastly a grandson of Tshekedi Khama is shown crossing the dry Limpopo river – the border between Botswana and South Africa – in the middle of the 1992 drought – while training to manage the Bamangwato Rhino Reserve.

Introduction

AUGUST 2004 SAW the fiftieth anniversary of my sailing out of Liverpool as a raw recruit for supposedly a lifetime in the Colonial Service. Within months we were told that we were no longer needed and I accepted early retirement and a modest lump sum at age 28. This book is a distillation of what I witnessed over the next 45 years of continuing to work and travel in Africa. It covers various topics concerned with the way African countries have fared in the struggle for independence. The 50 years cover periods under settler governments, colonial rule, transition and full independence. My wife, Theresa, and I have worked in 12 countries and visited another 12 over the past 50 years. We met at the Quaker London Yearly Meeting in 1958 and married a year later in Jordans Friends Meeting House where William Penn was buried after his death in 1718.

We do not claim to have made a special contribution but have an unusual breadth of experience due to our movement between countries and jobs. This is one of the inevitable results of the policy of Africanisation pursued after majority rule. While it ensured wider employment opportunities for Africans it also led to some too rapid promotions and the loss of valuable expatriate skills. We have enjoyed our varied careers and the opportunities we have had to share in some exciting and positive developments. While Africa still has an overall bad press we believe this is often undeserved and hope the book brings out some of the positive aspects of the past 50 years. In retirement and now based in Wales we thank those Africans who we have worked with for their friendship and for being, on the whole, positive to us. We wish them and their families well in their future challenges. Hopefully, the observations that are made in this book on Africa's record from 1954 – 2004 will have some bearing on the various meetings concerned with Africa in 2005.

While our careers have been disrupted by the needs of a growing family, in particular education, we have maintained a fairly unbroken contact with the continent. Where we have moved on too quickly this has been compensated to some extent by the breadth of jobs we have undertaken and the range of African people we have met and worked with. The appendices show the countries we have worked in over the 50 years. In all cases we have overall positive memories, even when living through events like Idi Amin's coup and the battle to "free" Rhodesia, when we were in Zambia. In looking for jobs we chose countries which were sufficiently stable for us to make a positive and long-term contribution. We hope that Quakers will be able to revive the service commitment that prevailed when they had The Friends Service Council (FSC) and later Quaker Peace and Service (QPS). I served on several committees of the former and was sent to West Darfur in the Sudan by QPS in 1988. While we appreciate some of the reasons we are sad at the dropping of service from the titles of BYM's central committees. We have always considered our work in Africa to be peace and service orientated.

The country we spent the longest time in was Zambia (11 years) and during 1980 – 86 we were involved with 2 part Quaker funded grass roots projects at Ibwe Munyama and the Gwembe Valley project of Harvest Help. (The former was the result of cooperation between QPS and the Salvation Army) We had 3 periods based in Wales[1] (1972-77 and 1986-89, 2000-2004) when one of us did consultancies in Africa for up to 2 months a year. The book is a memoir rather than an autobiography and the chapters are based on separate topics. A major aim is to balance the negative image of Africa given by many Western journalists with a more positive, rounded and sympathetic view. We would hope that our experiences will encourage others to pursue careers in African countries. One of the urgent tasks of the Commission on Africa is to develop a corps of service orientated specialists to back up future projects.

Both Theresa and I were inspired by experiences when, before we had met, we worked in Uganda and Nigeria. We met first at the London Yearly Meeting of Quakers in 1958 after a full session on Africa at a time when African colonies were rapidly moving towards independence. We sailed from Southampton to Cape Town in September 1959, bought a VW on arrival and drove via Basutoland to Serowe in what was then Bechuanaland. I had been recruited in London by Seretse and Tshekedi Khama to be Tribal Agricultural Officer to their tribe, the Bamangwato. The Resident Commissioner, the late Sir Peter Fawcus, who we met in the Imperial Reserve in Mafeking, said he hoped we would act as a bridge to get over the disruption following Seretse's marriage to Ruth Williams. Like many of our jobs it didn't last beyond the 2-year contract and nearly all my roles were taken over by central government. Serowe and Botswana gave us a wonderful introduction to working together in Africa. Theresa had to develop her own health centre in Serowe as the government said they did not employ women doctors.

Towards the end of the 50 years Theresa would find a job while I was self-employed as a journalist, occasional consultant, teacher and TV presenter. In between we worked most frequently as teachers of medicine and agriculture. For much of the time we earned local salaries while in Zambia alternately one received a British government supplement. Our most satisfying periods were in Uganda at Makerere University and in Zambia. In both cases I trained a counterpart to take over my job. Theresa repeatedly had to resign her community medicine posts so that we could move on together. In between these moves we raised a family of three – Marguerite Joan Mabathuse(born 1960 in Bulawayo, Rhodesia), Kageha Jeruto (born 1961 in Vihiga, Kenya and adopted 1965) and Jeremy Peter (born 1966 in Eastbourne). Kageha was one of several badly malnourished and sick babies in the Friends Hospital, Kaimosi, Kenya. Theresa was in charge of the children's ward and saw a need for fresh air and closer human contact – so they were fostered for weeks or months in our home.

In several of the countries where we worked there were no other Quakers but wherever possible we have joined local meetings or when travelling, visited outlying Friends. From 1959 – 61, when we lived in Serowe, Bechuanaland (now Botswana) we became deeply involved in the evacuation of those escaping the State of Emergency which followed the Sharpeville Massacre in South Africa (see Chapter VIII). Guy Clutton-Brock moved near with his wife after being released from prison in Rhodesia. We visited his widow, Molly, during 2004 in North Wales where she has been an attender at Ruthin Friends Meeting.

Throughout our first 25 years in Africa we were regularly visited by travelling Quakers. During 1977-80 these included the team assigned to make regular visits to the branches of the Zimbabwe Patriotic Front. They were led by Walter Martin of FSC and included Tony Gilpin and Trevor Jepson. Once Zimbabwe's Independence was achieved we helped to re-establish Central African General Meeting. Later in 1984 we hosted Hendrik Van Der Merwe of Cape Town Friends Meeting and joined him in a discussion with President Kaunda which led to one of the first links between the African National Congress and Afrikaner politicians. (See Chapter VIII)

Interaction with other Quaker yearly meetings started when we moved to Friends Africa Mission, Kaimosi, Kenya in January 1962. We were part of an influx of mainly British teachers, part funded by overseas aid. The original mission had been founded in 1902 by Quakers from Friends United Meeting based in Richmond, Indiana, USA. As Kenyan independence approached more American Friends were recruited from East coast yearly meetings to produce more qualified Kenyans. We maintained contacts with Kaimosi while Theresa taught at Moi University in 1995-6. I gave a series of 10 lectures at Friends Theological College. We were welcomed back at Kaimosi in 2004 while Theresa taught for three months at TICH in Kisumu. We are currently conveners of the Friends Africa Interest Group, an informal group of Britain Yearly Meeting. Our preparative meeting is, at the time of writing, pursuing a concern to raise support for the Friends Hospital, Kaimosi on a long-term basis.

While in many respects this book is written from a Quaker angle we would emphasise that we have always acted from an ecumenical and multi-faith position. In Nigeria I was the Senior Friend Secretary of the Student Christian Movement. Later I was briefly a consultant for the World Council of Churches. In South Africa, when far from a Quaker meeting, we alternately attended services of the Methodist and Anglican Communities in Mtunzini, near Richards Bay. During the first Iraq war we helped to organize a demonstration with the Zimbabwe Fellowship of Reconciliation (FOR) and made contact with local Muslims. Briefly we replaced the British High Commissioner and American Ambassador as tennis partners of the Iraqi Ambassador!

The Christian Rural Fellowship of East Africa (CRFEA) was formed after a conference in Kikuyu, Kenya in 1967. Members came from a wide range of Protestant and Catholic missions and churches. The book New Hope for Rural Africa (Edited by E. R. Watts and published by E.A. Publishing House (.1968 Nairobi), guided CRFEA until its dissolution in the late 1970s when travel became too difficult.

Peace activities since the 1970s have included membership of the International Physicians for the Prevention of Nuclear War and SERVAS. The former involved meetings we attended in 'Iron Curtain' countries such as Hungary (1984), Moscow (1987) plus one in Japan (Hiroshima 1989). SERVAS members were contacted in Budapest, Moscow and Japan. While in Zambia I became SERVAS secretary from 1982-86. We were introduced to SERVAS, which promotes international visitation, by Quakers in Oxford and have since found out that many Quakers are SERVAS hosts.

NOTE

1. In 1968, while on leave from Uganda, we bought the hill farm Maes-yr-eglwys (Church meadow) in the Swansea Valley. It was uninhabitable and for our 1970 leave we lived in a caravan. A Quaker architect in Swansea agreed to design and supervise the restoration of the house before our return in 1972. In our absences the house was let to local people while the sheep were farmed by a partner in the village – Tom Pritchard.

Acknowledgements

THE BOOK IS mainly based on shared experiences with my wife Theresa from 1959 onwards. I prefer to write long hand and she has checked chapters at various stages and made many suggestions. Word processing was done in South Africa by Elaine van Westhuizen of Mtunzini, Kwa Zulu Natal. Responsibility for errors remain mine.

Throughout our 50 years in Africa, but particularly up to 1980, we have been blessed with regular visits from mainly British Quakers They included:-

Jack Catchpool, Philip and Myrtle Radley, Leslie Smith, Robert Pearl, Mary and Bernard Lawson, Ross Wood, Phyllis and Kenneth Southall, David and Frances Murray-Rust, Christopher and Hannah Taylor, John and Alma Harding, Alastair Heron, Simon and Jane Fisher and Martin Wilkinson. These and others gave us support in the spirit of the Quaker tradition of travelling in the Ministry. (Ref – Quaker Faith and Practice 13-20). Other visitors are mentioned in the text.

Many of the influences on my thoughts date from student days in Reading, London and Oxford as well as from when I was SCM Senior Friend Secretary in Nigeria. I have had recent contacts with Nelson Nwosu of Nigeria, Victor Anomah Ngu of Cameroon, Donald Thomas of Nairobi all of whom I knew in the 1950s.

Since returning to Wales in 1999 we have been convenors of the Friends Africa Interest Group and are indebted to those Quakers who have supported us in a variety of ways. We hope the book will help to keep Africa in the thoughts of a wide range of people in Africa, Britain and the United States.

The following organisations in Britain have helped us keep in touch with some of the countries where we worked. Addresses are given in case others would like to contact them:-

Dolen Cymru (Lesotho), 128 The Exchange, Mount Stuart Sq., Cardiff CF10 5ED

Harvest Help (Zambia & Malawi), 3-4 Old Bakery Row, Wellington, Telford TF1 1PS

Farmers Overseas Action Group (FOAG – Uganda), Ridgeway Farm, Powick, Worcester WR2 4SN

Africa Now (Kenya), 3 Collins Street, Oxford OX4 1XS

The Britain – Nigeria Association, 2 Vincent Street, London SW1P 4LD

Britain-Tanzania Society, c/o 24 Oakfield Drive, Reigate, Surrey RH2 9NR

APT Enterprise Development, 29 Northwick Business Centre, Moreton-in-Marsh, Glos. GL56 9RF

Quaker Peace and Social Witness, Friends House, Euston Road, London NW1 2BJ (Uganda & S. Africa)

Britain-Zimbabwe Society, c/o 5a Crick Road, Oxford OX2 6QJ

Hands around the World, P.O. Box 62, Lydney, Gloucestershire GL15 6WZ

Zambia Society, 4 Ashurst Way, East Preston, Littlehampton BN16 1AG

Footnote

The publication of this book has been hastened because of its possible relevance to the Commission on Africa. The author apologises for any infringements of copyright which may have occured as a result.

CHAPTER I

Under Africa's Spell

"WHITE MAN COME" – What for? – it was a question shouted out by a small boy in the mountain village of Bafut in Cameroon, West Africa. I was passing in a Land Rover as a consultant to an international organization in Rome. There was no time to even shout a quick riposte let alone an answer to the question as our vehicle enveloped the small crowd of villagers in dust. But it is a question that has been asked for over a hundred years in thousands of villages throughout Africa. The answers that the village elders would give the small boy have probably not changed significantly since the days of colonialism. Europeans are still seen in Africa as the people with money, power and as the main source of aid.

This incident took place in 1989. I had been under Africa's spell since going to Reading University in 1950. There I met a group of Nigerian students being prepared for the soon to be discussed hand over of power by the British. Since those post-war days thousands of white men and women have come under a similar spell while working with Africans as teachers, doctors, nurses, administrators or in business. They have gone out as volunteers, under aid contracts, as missionaries and, in my case in Bafut, as international consultants.

Very few of my fellow agriculturalists have been able to follow an almost continuous career in Africa since the 1950's. In my case it has been possible largely because of my wife and her career as a doctor. As a medical student in University College, London and the London Hospital, she met few African students. But the fact that she did her pre-registration training in Uganda immersed her in Africa. Unlike me she became proficient in both Ki-Swahili and

1

Luganda. Many of her friends were Tanzanian doctors and she visited and stayed in their homes in Sukuma villages south of Mwanza, on Lake Victoria. As a rare single European woman she was invited to a range of events both at Government House and the Kabaka's Palace. The four Kings of Uganda stood in line for a photo-opportunity on one occasion! She returned to Britain under the spell of Africa and we met at the Quaker Yearly Meeting in 1958 when an entire session was devoted to African issues. After we had both spoken during the session we met for a cup of coffee to share our enthusiasm.

Having enrolled in Her Majesty's Colonial Service in 1953 I spent a year training to be a Rural Education Officer in Nigeria. Fortunately I was able to get a room in No. 1 Hans Crescent in Knightsbridge, London – just behind Harrods. This was a British Council hostel for overseas students, mainly from Africa, and provided a wonderful complement to our course in Senate House. One day a week we crossed the road for language study at the School of Oriental and African Studies. My language was Hausa, but to my great disappointment I was re-posted to a Yoruba speaking area a day before our ship docked in Lagos. It was at No. 1 Hans Crescent that I became friendly with a student, Victor Ngu, from the then Cameroon UN Trusteeship territory – near the village of Bafut. Victor and friends from Kenya were invited to our wedding in 1959 at Jordans Friends Meeting House.

The shrill voice of the small boy in Bafut had a questioning tone. It naturally led to my wondering what he made of the steady stream of white men, and increasingly women, passing through his village. I had previously visited Bafut in 1955 in the wake of Gerald Durrell whose book 'Bafut Beagles' had an amusing account of the whisky loving Fon of Bafut. Gerald Durrell, in his various books about his animal collecting expeditions showed that he came under the spell of Africa and made many repeat visits.

In 1989 a major difference was that I was employed by the International Fund for Agricultural Development, IFAD, based in Rome. The leader of our appraisal team was an African woman Madame Diop: an international consultant, from Senegal. Our expert on credit and cooperatives was Dr. Reddy from India. In the intervening years what used to be the UN trusteeship of West Cameroon had been combined with French ruled, East

2

Cameroon., to form the Republic of Cameroon. My close student friend during 1953-54 in London, Victor Anomah Ngu, had just retired as Minister of Health in Yaounde after a glittering career as a surgeon and Vice-Chancellor of the University. Under the guidance of a British teacher when at school Victor had come under the spell of classical music. We were able to walk from our hostel to the Royal Albert Hall. On one occasion I played in a mainly African football team in Hyde Park – for the British Empire versus the Rest of the World!

Victor Ngu's father, who I visited during the 1955 Bamenda Agricultural Show, was a remarkable man. Before the First World War he was employed by the German administration as an interpreter. He retained an affection for the Germans and must have had a sneaking hope that they would win the Second World War. He told me that under the British Bamenda people became less disciplined and respectful of authority. The amusing part was that when I questioned Victor about his memories of colonial days, he made the same criticism of the French that his father made of the British! Bamenda is situated high in the mountains and when I returned in 1989 I found it still spell binding in spite of the crowded streets.

A remarkable feature of the Bamenda area is the continued use of Pidgin English. In 1989 I was entertained by a highly educated Bamenda family all of whom were fluent in English, French and their local language. On going into the kitchen I was surprised to find the mother and her daughters were speaking in Pidgin! They explained that this was the language of the home and it reminded them of their childhood. At night they would tell stories in Pidgin. According to my bible for traveling in the 1950's, "Inside Africa", by John Gunther, there is a 'legend' that German universities taught courses in Pidgin in the days of their Empire!

Although Gerald Durrell's book the Bafut Beagles was popular in Cameroon people in the village itself were not so keen. He made fun of their king, the Fon, and his 70 wives. In fact I was told that many were very old and were inherited widows from his father and grandfather. In 1949 when Durrell first visited Bafut the British District Officer described him as "the most delightful old rogue" and advised that the "surest way to his heart is to prove to him that you can carry your liquor". Perhaps when I visited in 1989 I didn't provide sufficient "lubrication" as advised by the DO. In any case Durrell was invited for a return visit in 1989 and must have been well under Africa's spell whether lubricated or not.

A remarkable little book by Donald Fraser, a Scottish missionary in Nyasaland at the end of the nineteenth century[1] has a concise passage on the spell of Africa:-

> "To Britain the appeal of Africa is specially strong. Pioneers, missionaries, traders, travellers, soldiers, civil servants, serried rank upon serried rank have flowed out from this tiny island kingdom, many of them to live and die for that far country. For all types of men Africa holds an abiding fascination. The student, the trader, the hunter, the philanthropist, firstly and lastly the evangelist, each and all have felt it, and in each case it differs. The riddle of the human race, its origin and development, the greed of gain, the desire of sport and adventure, the love of fellowmen, the sense of the mysterious, the awful responsibility of millions of souls still ignorant of Christ. All this is embodied in Africa and has its significance for the readers of her story".

The range of people attracted to Africa hasn't changed much over the past 100 years. Even then it was attractive to Asians who found it a good place to trade. Lebanese merchants operated along the West African coast and Greeks monopolized trade in Rwanda and Burundi under Belgian rule. Missionaries in certain missions, such as the American Quakers who went to Kenya in 1902, may have reduced in numbers. They have been more than made up by the escalating number of American evangelical groups. When we went to our local supermarket in Eldoret, Kenya in 1995-6 Kenyans would sometimes be outnumbered by missionaries. Even hunters when banned in one country seem to find another where hunting is opening up. However, while there seems a plentiful supply of westerners willing to spend a few years in Africa, few develop a lifetime commitment nowadays.

One of the tragedies of Africa is the number of foreign people who are attracted by the scenery, the wide open spaces, the birds, the climate or the wildlife but do not relate to the indigenous people or learn to like them. Many of these expatriates only stay in Africa for relatively short periods while they make a film or write a book. An example of someone who fell under the spell and stayed to contribute to the country of his choice was Sir Michael Blundell of Kenya. His memoir published in 1994 was entitled "A Love Affair with the Sun – a memoir of 70 years in Kenya".

Kenya has, in spite of recent problems with terrorism and corruption, one of the most successful and stable economies in Africa. Compared to the rest of the continent it is extremely poorly endowed with minerals or oil deposits. Yet if has provided a favourable place for those who have come under Africa's spell and have wished to stay for a lifetime. Sir Michael Blundell came out in 1924 to be a farmer. He moved into politics and was Minister of Agriculture before independence. This post was filled by white settlers in Zimbabwe and Kenya after independence – Dennis Norman in Zimbabwe and Bruce McKenzie in Kenya. They all 3 performed useful roles at difficult times. Many of those coming under the spell leave, like Karen Blixen of 'Out of Africa' fame, because of responsibilities in their country of birth. In our own case our 3 children and the responsibility of the Welsh farm were big factors in our overcoming the spell. Since 1999, when we returned to the farm, we have however made visits to South Africa (2x), Zimbabwe (2x), Botswana, Namibia, Kenya (2x) and Tanzania. A tragedy happened in South Africa when we lived at Mtunzini on the KwaZulu Natal coast from 1996-1999. We had been introduced to a European couple in another part of the country who we were told would like to meet us because of our East African experiences. We phoned them and they were keen to come and see us. Within a week both were attacked in a house on the farm where they had worked until retirement. The husband died almost immediately but his wife was left paralysed for life.

In our telephone conversation I was told that the retired farmer and his wife had just returned from visiting relatives in Britain. The farmer wanted to return because the South African climate and outdoor life suited him. His wife said she was nervous about returning and wanted to stay in Britain. She was over-ruled by her husband who despite loving the South African life style "hated black people". It was sad that he had not come under a wider African spell.

For some time there has been an on-going debate in South Africa between the Government and farmer's representatives over the growing number of farm murders. The figure quoted in the 18 July 2003 issue of the *Farmers Weekly* is given as 1 400. There are claims that these are part of a genocide campaign but there is little evidence that they are coordinated. The KwaZulu-Natal case would seem to have been motivated by a grudge of a former employee. The case for claiming centrally organized violence would seem much stronger in Zimbabwe where most farm invasions were opposed by farmer's work forces who rarely benefited from the 2000-2002 invasions. Most invasions involved threats by mobs and there were relatively few deaths.

In my own case I was fortunate that I got to know a range of people from African countries before I set foot in Africa and came under a wider African spell. As a consequence I resisted the idea of becoming a settler and saw myself as someone who was there to help and work with indigenous people. Most missionary societies insist on their missionaries retiring at 60 or 65 to return to the country where they were recruited.

After both world wars the temptation to be a settler and acquire a farm was strong. In the 1950's there were regular advertisements in the *British Farmer's Weekly* for assisted settlement schemes in Northern Rhodesia (now Zambia). When we visited Zimbabwe soon after it gained independence in 1980 farms and houses could be bought at knock-down prices following the exodus caused in part by President Mugabe's victory in the first election. Even amongst the Quakers we met when we attended the Harare and Bulawayo meeting houses in 1958-61, and after the ceasefire in 1980, there were a few sympathizers with the settler controlled governments. When we visited the flat of one family before the 1980 election we discovered they were ready packed to leave as soon as they heard that Robert Mugabe had won. Their prediction of a complete collapse in the economy took 20 years to materialize.

The spell of Africa for those of European descent is quite understandable. Elderly missionaries who have spent perhaps 50 years working amongst people in an area that has become home are understandably reluctant to return to the rigours of Europe or North America. One American Quaker missionary, Edith Ratcliff, who died during 2003 aged 86 in Kenya went out as a nurse in 1946. She was so determined to die in Kenya that she rarely left the country and for years used her coffin as a coffee table to make the point. A British Rural Education Officer, Mr. G.N. Herington in Nigeria, who I lived with for 3 months in Ibadan, lost his first wife to Yellow Fever in the 1930's. He planned to retire near Ibadan, and built a house with 2 identical wings for himself and his trusted servant Jeremiah. His plans changed when he re-married and he died eventually in Britain. Edith Ratcliff built a house in 1984 in the compound of Meshach Mudamba. At her huge funeral he described her as his "blood sister".

Will the spell of Africa continue to draw Europeans and Americans to spend much of their lives there? Undoubtedly there is a steady flow of tourists and the "War against Terrorism" in the Middle East has to some extent led to more tourists choosing African destinations. Kenyan tourism has suffered severely from the Nairobi and Mombasa terrorist attacks. In recent years work visas and citizenship have become harder to get. "Affirmative action" by the South African Government has led to an outflow of doctors, teachers and others of European descent. On the other hand the new policy known as NEPAD – The New Economic Plan for African Development – should lead to a flow of people from western countries to work in Africa. In one sense it is a renewal of David Livingstone's appeal to students at Cambridge. When he was about to return for his last journey he appealed to them. "I go back to Africa to try to make an open path for commerce and Christianity: do you carry out the work which I have begun; I leave it with you". Livingstone's career switch from missionary to explorer was a sign of his coming under a wider African spell and his realization that there could be no progress while slavery still existed.

The "path of commerce" that followed Livingstone's speech had some undesirable consequences. Slavery took many years to be extinguished and even today there are vestiges of slavery. While the African states who have backed NEPAD are searching mainly for investment that will generate jobs there must inevitably be an influx of people from other countries with technical and financial skills. The idea that all the oil wells, mines, factories and farms in Africa would be run by indigenous people was never realistic. Business in most countries is accepted as involving people from many nationalities. African countries will need to welcome this and it is inevitable that some will fall under the spell of Africa and wish to settle. Immigration rules will have to be more relaxed if NEPAD is to work.

7

A remarkable recent example of someone coming under the spell of Africa comes from Botswana. A Scottish law professor, Alexander McCall Smith has produced a string of best selling books as a result of his experiences in, what on the face of it, seems an unlikely part of Africa. When we lived in Botswana, then the Bechuanaland Protectorate, from 1959-61, just after we had married, it was one of the poorest countries in Africa. In retrospect the people of Botswana were lucky that Cecil Rhodes did not know the country was rich in diamonds and had reserves of coal, copper, nickel and other minerals. The books focus on an "African Miss Marple" figure Precious Ramotswe. What is new in writings about Africa is that McCall Smith manages to enthuse his readers about African values and customs. McCall Smith admits to having been enthralled by his experiences in Botswana and has helped many in the United States and Europe to appreciate Africa.

When we left Botswana it had only two tiny strips of tarmac in Lobatse and Francistown. The capital Gaborone was then still a small village. The fact that it is now one of Africa's most successful economies is not just a question of discovering diamonds. Angola and Congo both discovered diamonds and huge oil reserves but have squandered their resources on inter-tribal fighting accentuated by Cold War arms supplies from West and East. Botswana's success is largely due to better political leadership and leaving the management of the economy in competent hands, sometimes expatriates – in many cases people like McCall Smith who came under the spell of Africa.

For both Theresa and I the spell of Africa came mainly from the people we worked with and the work we were able to do. Africanisation was never a great threat as we understood before taking a job that we were there to train someone to take over. The climate was never a major attraction as neither of us particularly enjoy hot weather. The later spells of wildlife and, for Theresa, the opportunity to swim in the Indian Ocean on our doorstep, came later after our children were at boarding schools or college. There was an extraordinary freedom to do things that would have been impossible in Britain. Theresa started one of the first mother and child clinics in Botswana using a house lent by Ruth Khama. In my case I was able to knock on the door of the Zambian state television centre and offer to research and present a weekly farming programme called Lima Time. This went on for several years after we left but an attempt to repeat the exercise in Zimbabwe never got the same official backing.

Our falling under the spell of African wildlife came for me in Nigeria during my second tour in 1957. With 3 friends from Ibadan I tracked a herd of elephants in a remote valley near the border of what is now Benin. We were led by a local hunter armed with a bow and arrow. After crossing the Ogun River we followed elephant tracks for at least 3 hours in fairly open tall Hyparrhenia grassland. Fortunately the elephants were in thick forest and we approached to within 10-15 metres before they heard us, trumpeted and took off – in the opposite direction from us. We have sought out elephants ever since in Uganda, Kenya, Tanzania, Botswana, South Africa and Malawi. Our best viewing was in the Addo Elephant Park in South Africa. For 3 hours we watched herd after herd approach a series of pools where they socialized, enjoyed mud baths and had lengthy drinks. We much prefer hides where animals and birds can be seen interacting in their own time without the hassle of a tour guide. Wherever one is in Africa there are always the birds which we have learnt to enjoy more and more. When we took 2 grand children to a park with hippo and rhino they got more enjoyment from watching the antics of squirrels. They were similar to the grey squirrels we enjoy in Wales. Hopefully our 5 grand children will pick up a bit of the spell of Africa from their visits to us plus the animals and birds they have seen on visits, as well as in photographs and slide shows.

NOTE
1. The Future of Africa by Donald Fraser, Young People's Missionary Movement. London 1911, page 3.

9

CHAPTER II

Settler or Expatriate

FOR THOSE WHO fall under Africa's spell today there are limited prospects for settlement and the acquiring of citizenship. Before the Independence of Zimbabwe and the achievement of majority rule in South Africa it was normal for immigrants to have one way tickets and eventually become citizens. In the 1950's I can remember seeing Government advertisements in the British *Farmers Weekly* to recruit farmers for the Mkushi Block in Northern Rhodesia. Assistance with passages was often available for settlers particularly in South Africa which was anxious to boost its white population. Prior to the Nationalist win in 1948 this assistance would have been mainly for English speakers. 51.8% of immigrants came from the UK between 1939-45 while this had dropped to 22.9% in 1979. During later years the percentage from the UK rose again presumably because of adverse publicity in countries like the Netherlands.[1]

My first encounter with settler communities in Africa was in 1952 when I was a student at Reading University. I went with a group of students to the Town Hall to hear Sir Roy Welensky campaigning for the British Government to back the proposal for a Central African Federation. Nelson Nwosu, a fellow agricultural student from Nigeria, who I have remained in contact with to this day, asked a challenging question. Sir Roy started his reply with: "I would like to thank my fellow African for that question!" He had been talking about "partnership" between black and white in the proposed federation. He wanted to show how open handed he was to Africans. The impact was however spoilt when he hesitated and added: "You are an African aren't you?"!

The Federation was strongly opposed by politically minded Africans because it was seen as a way of extending the existing settler ruled government in Southern Rhodesia to cover Northern Rhodesia and Nyasaland. I joined my African friends, who were mainly from West Africa, in opposing the Federation. When I returned to Britain in 1958 after 4 years in Nigeria, I joined the campaign to break up the Federation and was involved in the organization of a private conference in Oxford. It was organized by a childhood friend, Colin Leys, and a fellow political scientist, Cranford Pratt, and led to the book "A New Deal in Central Africa".[2] My small role was to host a Nyasaland delegate, Kanyama Chiume for a day. He subsequently fell out with President Banda of Malawi and lived the rest of his life in exile in Tanzania.

Inevitably in the 1950's we could have been described as "anti-settler". However once settler rule ended in Kenya, Zimbabwe and other countries we had many settler friends. A Quaker student friend, Donald Thomas, who was studying Agriculture at Cambridge while I was at Reading, acquired a farm in Kenya at about the time of independence. He later became a citizen and still lives in Nairobi after retiring as a professor in the University. Another Quaker, Derek Archer with whom we stayed in Salisbury in January 1980, stayed on. During the 3 months when the Union Jack flew again and Lord Soames was briefly Governor our friend worked for the City Council. He and his wife Edith soon moved to the Eastern Highlands to a store and farm when he saw he would not be able to continue as a civil servant. He became the leading expert in growing the exotic flower, Protea, and provided many jobs for the neighbouring communal area. He helped to organize and fund famine relief in the area during a drought.

When Zimbabwe gained Independence on April 18 1980 we were living in neighbouring Zambia. There were temptations to move to Zimbabwe as property values declined. In spite of the early land reform farms could still be bought if government provided a letter to show they were not interested. In retrospect our decision to stay in Zambia until 1986 and then move to the UK until 1990 was a wise one. A major factor was my continued feeling that acquiring land in a country altered one's attitudes towards the people, government and even neighbours. In 1968, when faced with an uncertain future working in African countries, we had acquired a

45 acre hill farm in South Wales. It was designed to be a bolt hole in case of coups or sudden Africanisation. Our protective attitude to having our own property was tested by finding that we had a bridle path going past our front door. It has never been used for at least 50 years but still appears on the Ordinance Survey maps as a Right of Way. As I write this in 2004 our appeal to the Rights of Way Officer of the Brecon Beacons National Park is still pending after being submitted in 2001. Our main case is that those who made the Definitive Map in the 1950's confused 2 former access routes to the farm with a public route.

That national identity feelings are magnified by alienation of land to another nationality applies in Wales as much as in Africa. It is expressed nowadays more in connection with the purchase of houses, particularly as second homes, by people from England. Our neighbouring Cnewr Estate in the Swansea Valley, once described as "the largest sheep farm in Europe", was "alienated" in 1819 when John Christie from England purchased the Crown Allotment of Brecknock. It was taken over by the McTurk Family who came with their Cheviot Sheep from Scotland in the 1850's. We bought our farm, Maes-yr-eglwys (Meadow of the Church) from the estate manager Mr. West who also came from Scotland to work for the McTurk's.

Additional reasons for buying a Welsh sheep farm revolved around my great love of Wales and the Welsh hills developed from childhood before and during the war when all our holidays were spent in Wales. From 1949-50 I worked on 2 Welsh farms as a conscientious objector to military service. At university I developed an interest in small-scale farming and worked as a migrant labourer in Switzerland and France. Maes-yr-eglwys enabled me to farm with a minimum of mechanization. We ran the farm with the use of only a wheelbarrow and hand tools. The water supply was from a natural spring and by gravity. A wood fired burner and a fuel wood plantation provided heat for the house. We were also able to use the farm's common rights on the Great Forest of Brecknock. This gave valuable experience of the problems involved in common grazing – a practice followed in nearly all African countries.

Land issues have played a major role in the recent history of a number of African countries. Alienation of land to settlers, and particularly the granting of freehold tenure, has contributed very substantially to the collapse of Zimbabwe's economy. Very few settlers took seriously the warning by Mr. Mugabe in 1987 that only the present generation of settlers were welcome to stay[3] in "the colonial lifestyle" they were accustomed to. The author, who based his book on extensive research in 1986-7 concluded that "in a generation or so the white population will have dwindled into insignificance". When in 1991-2 I spoke to branches of the Commercial Farmers Union on the redistribution of land I had witnessed in Kenya (1962-72) and Zambia (1977-86) no one seemed to take this warning seriously.

At Lancaster House in 1979 the British Government had resisted the idea of a redistribution scheme on Kenyan lines – presumably because they found it would be too costly. The Zimbabwe Government was bound by the agreement to operate a "willing seller-willing buyer" policy but hadn't sufficient funds to make a major dent in the exclusive white ownership of much of the best land in Zimbabwe. Invasions by "war veterans" has proved to be a very counter-productive method of redistribution. Fortunately there hasn't yet been a total exodus of expatriate commercial farmers as occurred in Uganda. If the present government is replaced or manages to adopt more constructive policies there is still (in 2003) a possibility that Zimbabwe's agricultural sector can be revived.

In the case of South Africa a situation as extreme as Zimbabwe's recent land invasions and evictions seems unlikely. Much of the alienated land was taken over 150 years ago as opposed to around 100 years ago in Zimbabwe. South Africa is more urbanized and people have been softened up by having pension schemes which provide a high percentage of rural income. It is still one of the few Sub-Saharan countries with an effective government pension for the elderly. Yet with unemployment at 30-40% and rising, a rural minimum wage of £65 and bursting informal settlements around towns ways need to be found to get more people on to land. The costs of buying out large numbers of commercial farmers are exorbitant. Other routes may be needed such as converting some freehold to leasehold as was done by the former President of Zambia, Kenneth Kaunda. Such an approach would mean taking seriously African sensibilities to land alienation.

On my first visit to what was then Southern Rhodesia in 1958 I was met from the Beira train at Rusape and stayed at St. Faiths Mission. Guy and Molly Clutton-Brock had founded a multi-racial farming community there. For his work for the growing African nationalist movement Guy became a revered figure after Independence. He was invited to settle back to Zimbabwe by Robert Mugabe but refused partly because he felt he would be a burden on the new state. Mugabe and Didymus Mutasa regularly traveled to North Wales to see the C-B's when they were in London. Guy is still the only white person to be commemorated in Heroes Acre, outside Harare.

After my visit I wrote to Guy from England for some career advice following my opting out of Her Majesty's Colonial Service. In a letter dated 18-6-58 he unexpectedly recommended buying a farm near St. Faith's or in Nyasaland. "I think it most important that Christians should come to S.R. and Central Africa ... to work on an independent basis as farmers". He even recommended "getting a job in the Native Ag. Dept. here". "Dudley Robinson (a Quaker) is a very good person and a great friend of ours here. He is about to be Director." Guy did not seem in principle to be anti-settler and actually became a citizen until he was deported by Ian Smith in 1970 and had his citizenship taken away.

In 1958 I was already committed to spending a year at St. Peters Hall, Oxford studying Agricultural Economics (plus finding a wife!) After completing the course I was recruited through the Clutton-Brocks support organization, the African Development Trust, to work in the Bechuanaland Protectorate. I was interviewed in the London Clinic by Tshekedi Khama shortly before his death. Theresa and I spent 2 years in Serowe where she started one of the first Public Health Clinics, having been told in the Imperial Reserve, Mafeking that they did not employ women! My post had the unique title Tribal Agricultural Officer and my boss was Seretse Khama – then secretary of the Bamangwato Tribal Administration. Guy was released from Salisbury prison after the banning of the African National Congress in 1959. He moved his base to Bechuanaland. He and Molly regularly stayed with us in Serowe while starting the communal farm at Radisele.

Botswana, as it was originally a protectorate not a colony, never had many settlers as in Zimbabwe. White farmers have been confined almost entirely to the 10 mile wide strip known as the Tuli Block, along the border with South Africa. While many white traders were supporters of the South African Government in the 1950's they quickly supported local political parties as independence approached. The High Commissioner for Botswana in London has for several years recently been Roy Blackbeard, son of the main garage owner in Serowe when we lived there from 1959-61.

A remarkable case of settler adaptation to the new realities comes from Kenya. Under the title "The Last Boer" the *South African Farmers Weekly* recently[4] featured Fanie Kruger who still farms outside Eldoret in Kenya. He has learnt to live with his neighbour, Nicholas Biwott, who has obtained many of the neighbouring, formerly white-owned, farms. Over a long period he has been a funder and supporter of the ruling party, the Kenya African Union – Kanu – but in 1997 led a blockade of the town to protest at low farm prices. Some former white farmers in Kenya have taken jobs as managers on farms they once owned. When we lived in Eldoret in 1995-6, while my wife was a professor at Moi University, one former farmer spent Saturdays in the Club signing in the guests of his boss – Nicholas Biwott.

It is easy to forget how entrenched settlers became at the height of white minority rule. Soon after Independence in Zimbabwe, Terence Ranger, Professor of Race Relations at St. Anthony's College unearthed a report[5] of the Provincial Native Commissioner dated 6 May 1957 on St. Faiths, Rusape. These are some extracts of the report:-

"With the Europeans at St. Faith's there is no colour bar, a feature highly unpopular in the district .... Natives, e.g. the Mission's lorry driver, eat in Clutton-Brock's at table with him, they even sleep in his house.... This is bad enough if the standard remained a high one, but it does not. Reputable Europeans who have visited the Clutton-Brocks state that .... The Native man who may be sitting in Clutton-Brock house does not on arrival of a European, rise from his seat .... To accommodate a Native child burnt on a farm in this District, the Native child slept in the Clutton-Brock's own daughter's bed, the daughter being away at boarding school".

15

It is perhaps not surprising that in Robert Mugabe's own tribute in the same publication he states: "When in the fullness of time, after our long and bitter struggle, I was called on to form the government of the newly independent Zimbabwe, the example of the Clutton-Brocks made it easier for us all to adopt our policy of reconciliation". Guy helped "to work out the first anti-racialist ANC Constitution which called for "the national unity of all the inhabitants of the country in true partnership of race, colour or creed". He also comments that "he was the only white to be arrested when Whitehead banned the ANC and detained over 500 of its members without trial". Perhaps recent events in Zimbabwe would have been less racially inspired if more of those 500 had been white. South Africa had a much wider mix in its opposition to Apartheid. Both the ANC and PAC had white, Asian and coloured supporters who suffered severely if they were arrested.

The extraordinary thing about Zimbabwe, in retrospect, is that the white community thought they had excellent race relations. They were not like the Apartheid ruled South Africans. When in 1990 we went to the University of Zimbabwe in Harare for my wife to work in the Medical School we were accommodated for a few weeks in the Jameson Hotel. Very often at dinner we bumped into a friendly couple of Scottish descent. They even persuaded us to join a Caledonian dancing group despite our English/Welsh origin! They repeatedly emphasized after hearing we came from countries to the north: "The natives here are very friendly, you will enjoy your time here!"

I don't think, in retrospect, we ever used the term 'native' which to us smacked of colonialism. However in the book on the Clutton-Brocks[6] the term is used in Robert Mugabe's tribute to the couple: "I did not meet the Clutton-Brocks until after I returned to the then Southern Rhodesia from Ghana in 1960". "I had heard about this unusual white couple who had come to St. Faith's Mission .... Who 'fraternised' with the natives in a way few other whites in those days did, and who not only talked about freedom and justice for all but worked towards that ideal both in the small community of St. Faith's and in the larger community of the country as a whole through the newly-emerging African nationalist groups".

If we had followed Guy's advice in his 1958 letter and become settlers would we have had the same impact? Probably not. The fact that he was the only white amongst the 500 arrested in 1959 implies that he was unique and that explains why he has got a place in Heroes Acre. Several Quakers, including Dudley Robinson, Stanley and Margaret Moore, John and Alma Harding, Roy Henson were close sympathizers with the cause of the nationalists. The Cold Comfort Farm Society Constitution designated "3 Europeans as chief members or shareholders"[7] to get around the racially based land laws. These were "the Bishop of Matabeleland, Kenneth Skelton, Lord Acton and Mr. Jack Grant".[8] They were not members of nationalist groups and it is doubtful whether we would have become members if we had tried to farm in Rhodesia on our own account.

Our main involvement with nationalist groups was in Bechuanaland where, on the advice and encouragement of the Serowe District Commissioner, Mr. Robinson, we helped to organize an air lift to Ghana of refugees from the 1960 Sharpeville emergency in South Africa. A problem for Quakers, who sympathized with the nationalist movement, was the gradual move towards a violent challenge to the Apartheid Government. In 1960 this came to a head when we were visited by Patrick Duncan, formerly of the South African Liberal Party. He came to Bechuanaland to look for a farm to use as a military base for the use of the Pan African Congress which he had recently joined. He had an intense argument with Theresa, then ill in bed, over the rights and wrongs of joining the "armed struggle". Our unwillingness to get closely involved because of our pacifism was a factor in our moving north to Kenya when my contract came to an end in September 1961. Much of my work was taken over by the central government as relations with the Bamangwato improved. They had been disrupted since the row over Seretse's marriage to "Surbiton typist" Ruth Williams on September 25 1948. This led to the exile of Seretse to London and the banishment of Tshekedi until August 1952.

Moving to Kenya opened up many new opportunities and we arrived at Kaimosi Friends Africa Mission near Lake Victoria in January 1962. On the way, driving our VW beetle from Serowe to Kampala, I had passed a convoy of Afrikaans speaking Kenyan farmers making their way south. They feared they would lose their farms before or after independence in the following year. The article about "The Last Boer", already mentioned, relates how Fanie

17

Kruger was born before this exodus. There was "blind panic" fuelled by Mau Mau and "the slaughter and rape of white nuns in the Belgian Congo" which by then had become Zaire. His father had gone to Pretoria in July 1960 but returned and applied for citizenship, bought farms "for nothing" and was given machinery by departing Boers.

Jan Erns Kruger told his son "If we want to keep our land, we must not step out of line; we must respect the black man and he will respect us". He also said, as a South African rancher in Queenstown, Eastern Cape, said to us in November 2003, that the government was welcome to have his land. Zimbabwe's farmers would have fared better if more ways of transferring land had been found in the 1980's. The Krugers and other white farmers in Kenya have survived partly because of schemes like the million acre scheme in Kenya which paid settlers in sterling for their farms so that they could move elsewhere and re-establish. Zimbabwe might have been saved from the disastrous land invasion policy if the British Government and the international community had financed more such programmes in the 1980's and 90's.

We attended almost the first use of the vast ZANU-PF Conference Hall in Harare. The event was a major classical music concert and was packed, almost exclusively, by white Zimbabweans. It was a sign of the gap between the races and for me that our Scottish friends assurance that "the natives are friendly" underestimated the gap and particularly the lack of empathy and respect by many white Zimbabweans for their fellows. There was a far seeing cartoon in humorous magazine Punch soon after the massive defeat of the British Army in the battle of Isandlwana in 1879. It showed a rather substantial John Bull on a stool with a Zulu warrior in full regalia and the slogan "Respect your enemies" on his shield. The fact that so few white settlers in Africa had the respect for their African neighbours shown by the Clutton-Brocks has sadly contributed to the decimation of the settler community in Zimbabwe. A major issue now is how to avoid a repetition in South Africa. At the major "Towards South Africa 2004" Conference held in Westminster in October 2003 I suggested to the Minister of Agriculture and Land Affairs, Thoko Didiza, that they should look into the possibility of some form of land nationalization. Probably fearing the effect that any positive response would have on investment, the main purpose of the Conference, she replied that it was not being considered.

In 1975 President Kaunda of Zambia nationalized land in commercial farming areas. Overnight freehold tenure was converted to leasehold tenure with the government becoming the owner. Very little research has been done on the effects of this policy and I could not find anyone in Zimbabwe willing to discuss it. The Zambian Act of Parliament (Conversion of Titles) Act of 1975 had the following major provisions: "As from 1st July 1975 all freehold titles including those held by commercial farmers were abolished and replaced by 100 year leases. All unutilized tracts of farm land were taken over by the state".[9] While something as extreme as that would have a drastic effect in South Africa, it could be done in stages or in one small area to start with. It would give the Government some ammunition to fight off its critics. Land alienation is going to remain a major issue and almost anything would be better than a Zimbabwe type solution.

As will be seen from the few details of our two careers we have remained expatriates. Our aim has been to provide a service that is needed. To find the right jobs and fit in the needs of our family we have had to be quite mobile. Our longest service was 12 years in Zambia but we have spent 6 years in Uganda, 6 in Kenya, 3 in South Africa and 2 in Botswana.[10] Short assignments have involved Tanzania, Namibia, Sudan, Ethiopia, Nigeria, Zaire, and Cameroon. In several jobs we have been Africanised where our contracts have been terminated to allow a national to take over. We don't regret our highly mobile careers and have and have only thanks for the experience we have enjoyed.

NOTES

1. Page 277 South African Yearbook 1986. Govt. Printer, Pretoria.
2. "A New Deal in Central Africa". Edited by Colin Leys and Cranford Pratt. Heinemann. London. 1960.
3. Page 222. State Politics in Zimbabwe by Jeffrey Herbst. University of Zimbabwe Publications 1990.
4. Article by Darren Taylor in S.African Farmers Weekly dated 26/12/03
5. P.78 in Guy & Molly Clutton-Brock. Longmans. Zimbabwe 1987.
6. Guy and Molly Clutton-Brock. Longman, Zimbabwe, 1987, page 131.

19

7. Page 125. Guy & Molly Clutton-Brock. Longman. Zimbabwe, 1987.
8. Page 125. Guy and Molly Clutton-Brock. Longman, Zimbabwe, 1987.
9. p. 308 in "Lusaka and its environs". Edited by Geoffrey J. Williams, Zambia Geographical Association, LUSAKA, 1986
10. The total here does not add up to 50 years. Before we married I had 4 years in Nigeria and Theresa was in Uganda for 2 years. We were based in Wales from 1972-76 and 1986-89 and had an agreement that I could do consultancies for a maximum of 2 months a year.

CHAPTER III

Africa and Religion

AFRICA, SOUTH OF the Sahara, is a great melting pot of religions and has been able to assimilate both Christianity and Islam. While some Africans take to these, for them new religions, very strictly, others can be very flexible. When I worked with the state television corporation, ZBC, in Harare I was assigned a driver. He told me that he had formerly worked for the Saudi Arabian Embassy. I asked whether he was a Muslim and he explained that he had converted for the duration of his job!

When the Millenium was being anticipated there was a competition on the BBC African Service for "The African of the Millenium". We were asked to write a short piece backing our choice. I chose James Ernman Kwegyir Aggrey of Ghana – or what was in his time the Gold Coast. He travelled throughout Africa promoting education at all levels. He was born in 1875 and died in 1927 so his life spanned parts of two centuries. "He preached a message of the fundamental unity of the human race".[1] He "often dwelt upon the African's capacity for religion and the higher elements in their indigenous faith". He claimed "All Africans are religious, intensely so". He developed the concept of the keys of a piano – "you can't play good music with the white keys alone: you must have the black ones too. God wants to play beautiful music with his white and black keys together". These sentiments fitted well with the Quaker beliefs I had imbibed while growing up as a Quaker in Bournville, Birmingham and at Sidcot School.

The Quakers in Southern Africa have a Yearly Meeting when they gather from as far afield as Zambia, Namibia and even Madagascar. Whenever possible we have attended these gatherings

21

In 1997 they met at Mora-a-pula School in Gaborone, Botswana. The keynote speaker was Gabriel Setiloane the author of "African Theology".[2] It was an attempt to correct a situation where Christians have for too long failed to recognize the basic spirituality of African peoples. Gabriel quoted Desmond Tutu who once said that many Africans feel they "have been brain washed" by missionaries. This criticism could be applied to many missions throughout Africa. The Quaker mission at Kaimosi in Kenya was established in 1902 on very similar lines to other evangelical churches in Africa. It was called the Friends Africa Industrial Mission and had a very practical emphasis. A sawmill was driven by water power and training was given in a range of skills. Later, in the 1960's, an agricultural extension programme was started which we visited recently in 2004. In the 1940's it was involved in controversy over a new "Holy Spirit Movement" sect – Dini Ya Msambwa. Although they took over "a number of symbols and customs from the Christian churches they remained basically a movement built on the foundations of the ancestors". "They were strongly opposed to the existing churches in their area, including Quakers".[3]

In many ways the Friends Africa Mission was successful and Kenya now has more Quakers than any other country in the world. Jomo Kenyatta, the first President, was visited when detained by the British by a Quaker delegation. Later he had a Quaker minister of education in his first cabinet. Shortly before the end of President Moi's rule he appointed Musalia Mudavadi as Vice-President and the current President Kibaki sent his son Anthony to the British Quaker School Sidcot in 1989. Nearly all Quakers come from Luhya[4] speaking areas. Many of the American Friends left after independence and handed over to what was called East Africa Yearly Meeting. Divisions, largely on ethnic lines, started to emerge. Division was spurred by disputes over property such as churches and schools. A Hindu Judge once said he was surprised to find Quakers opposing each other in court. He told them Quakers were known for resolving disputes peacefully. The case was dismissed and they were told to go away and pray and only come to court if they failed to resolve the issue!

In 2004 we were welcomed at the Friends Theological College on the site of the Kaimosi Friends Africa Mission where we worked from 1962-65. That was a period of immense change since independence from Britain was achieved on 12 December 1963. The area was intensively researched by an anthropologist between 1954 and 1956.[5] He reveals that when the American Quaker missionaries were given their 1000 acre plot by the British District Commissioner they were taking on a lot of problems for the future. North Nyanza had 22 tribes, and the 1000 acres at Kaimosi was surrounded by land of the Tiriki. The missionaries had more converts in a neighbouring area where the land belonged to the Marogoli. In 1932, following a dispute with the neighbouring Chief Amiani, he "resigned from the Friends Church and joined the Salvation Army" (page 133). When we moved there 30 years later we employed a Salvation Army cook – Pedro. The Salvation Army had missions in many urban areas and quickly acquired a national status.[6] Quakers have remained, until very recently, confined to tribes from the Western Region. The failure to make a national Quaker church derives from the tribal division of members in what are called yearly meetings. Most of these are affiliated to Friends United Meeting in Richmond, Indiana, USA. In 2004 we noted encouraging signs that a few Quakers now come from non-Luhya speaking areas such as Nandi, Kisii, Turkana and Samburu.

Amongst the lesser known acts of President Idi Amin, following his coup in January 1971, when we were living in Uganda, was his decision to make Christians more united. He made one of his speeches when he attacked Christians for having too many branches. He gave a deadline for them to decide whether they were to be members of the Catholic Church or the Church of Uganda – part of the Anglican Communion. This edict applied to Quakers, of which there were three sections: around Mount Elgon, in Kampala (mainly Kenyans in the Uganda Police), and some Luhya speaking farmers on a colonial settlement scheme in the north. Uganda's economy was already in free fall so that many had already moved to Kenya and others followed.

In a sense Idi Amin was right: Christians and even Quakers are too divided. In the Kaimosi area there were Pentecostal missions from overseas who did not speak to each other. However there was a very active Christian Council of Kenya (CCK) in which Quakers played an important role. I used to write for their newspaper Rock and once wrote an article entitled "Negative Christianity" because of the long list of things Christians were told not to do such as drink alcohol, dance etc. I felt that most of Christ's teachings involved doing positive things. A particularly contentious issue was polygamy where a convert was expected to choose one wife and send the others away. Probably the biggest failure of missions was in developing a new sexual morality to replace the ones they swept away. The CCK was active in promoting the training of farmers as part of moves to resettle the former White Highlands. It played a crucial role in Kenya both before and after independence. Two of the Farmers Training Centres at Lugari and North Kinangop were partly staffed by Quakers.

On my African journey in 1958 I sailed in the M/S General Mangin, a Belgian ship, from Lagos, Nigeria to Pointe Noire near the mouth of the River Congo. We anchored off Port Gentil, downstream from Dr. Albert Schweitzer's famous mission at Lambaréné. Although today his attitudes would be seen as very paternal and even colonial he had a very deep respect for nature and a strong desire to serve African people. Archbishop Ndungane of Cape Town recently quoted him in relation to Ubuntu. "If (all) life is not regarded as intrinsically valuable, then man's relations to nature and his fellow man will dissolve". Ndungane goes on: "In the African world view, land has a deep religious significance. It is land that connects the unborn, the living and the dead ... We are all part of this fragile interdependent chain of life". The failure to appreciate the cultural importance of land is perhaps a key factor in the misjudgment by many Zimbabwean and South African whites of African attachment to the land of their ancestors. A missionary, working in Kenya, Father Kizito, visited Lambaréné in 1971 7 years after Schweitzer's death. Writing in the Sunday Nation[7] he quoted a Cameronian film director, Bassek ba Kobhio as saying "we blame Schweitzer for having joined our hell only in order to gain his heaven". He was "pushed only by his dedication to the people. That dedication I respect .... Yet if he has given a lot, he did not share". Kizito comments that he "had a total disregard for the culture of the people he served" although he "spoke with ease 6 European languages". He added that he "could not say a word in a local language"! As a very poor linguist myself I have some sympathy with Schweitzer – I don't even speak Welsh! Language versatility seems to be an area where Africans excel over Europeans. I also sympathise with Schweitzer's emphasis on service as a valid motive for working as a missionary.

During my first two tours in Africa, when I was a member of Her Majesty's Colonial Service in Western Nigeria, I interacted at weekends with staff and students of what was then the University College, Ibadan. As a student I had been active in the Student Christian Movement. I was soon asked to take on a voluntary role as Senior Friend Secretary of the Student Christian Movement of Nigeria. Several students and staff became friends and I am still in touch with Elnora Ferguson, widow of John Ferguson, who later was Head of the Selly Oak Colleges in Birmingham where thousands of missionaries have been trained. Another was Geoffrey Parrinder, author of the book "African Mythology".[8] This still provides an excellent introduction with some remarkable illustrations. One particularly striking one is a miniature bronze jug from "the Greek culture of Alexandria" dated "between the third and first centuries B.C." It could only have been modeled by a young woman from the middle of Africa. There is a striking resemblance to the 13th and 16th century AD bronze heads from Ifé and Benin in Nigeria. Her demeanour is not that of a slave and she has a most elaborate and presumably expensive hair do. It is a remarkable head and even more remarkable is the fact that people in Britain well after that time were being sought as slaves by the Romans and later by the people of North Africa.

Geoffrey Parrinder, who was Reader in the Comparative Study of Religions at Kings College, University of London, lived in West Africa for 20 years. African myths he describes (page 15) as "philosophy in parables". They "express joy in life and human activity". "It is a 'world affirming' philosophy in which life is thought of as good, despite human suffering, sex is to be enjoyed, and children are the gift of God". This perhaps explains why most Africans find it difficult to take on concerns over rapid population growth seriously. Noni Jabavu in her book "The Ochre People"[9] relates a conversation between her uncles over family limitation. They took off a white doctor's comments: "But we doctors are always telling you Kaffirs: 'there is that civilized device, birth control', ... Why not reduce yourselves to three millions, instead of these troublesome twelve'?" This was followed by a great mirth. "They looked around at each other and roared, for the very idea of family limitation is about as acceptable to Xhosa minds as a jackal in a sheep pen". Restrictions on the enjoyment of sex are still an issue for Christian churches in Africa and are at the core of the campaigns to reduce the spread of HIV, the virus causing AIDS. The almost universal dislike of the male condom is a related issue and as I write there is a campaign to make the Femidom or female condom more available, cheaper and acceptable.

Missions are of course gradually modifying the old paternalism and antagonism for indigenous cultures in Africa. However the Catholic and some evangelical churches have taken an extremely paternal view to the use of condoms. Due to the US Republican party dependence on the Mid West church vote this has even influenced government policy as regards aid to African countries in their campaigns to control AIDS. This is not to say that condoms should be promoted amongst young people. There is no reason why condom promotion for the sexually active cannot be combined with a campaign for faithful relationships amongst both the very young and the entire population. Anti-retrovirals, which have been promoted since the mid 1990's, are unlikely to bring the syndrome under control on their own. Those on anti-retrovirals are still infective, so without intense counseling may be responsible for spreading the virus further. The virginity campaigns being promoted by some evangelical churches in the USA have historical parallels in Africa. When I joined a UNICEF funded school Zimbabwe AIDS education campaign in 1992 I was quite unexpectedly assigned the cultural section. I tried to draw on the research of Dr. Michael Gelfand[10] who studied the culture of Shona people. He identified the great care taken by families to promote faithful relations and avoid early vaginal sex. In all the cultures I've studied relatives have a critical role in instruction on sexual matters. In the case of girls, maternal aunts seem to have had a much greater role than mothers. A group of Zulu mothers in Ngwelezane, Zululand told me in 1998 that they were unable to advise their daughters on sexual matters.

Churches, both of the traditional and the indigenous or separatist types, have a huge role to play in bringing the AIDS crisis under control. We were in Zambia when we first heard about this new infection through a video distributed by the Centre for Disease Control in Atlanta, Georgia, USA. The medical students that I joined to see the video in 1982 reacted negatively to the suggestion that it came from Africa. An early confusion was that it was thought to be mainly a problem for homosexuals. A newly qualified doctor, Dr. Kristina Baker, quickly saw the need to change behaviour by starting the Zambian Anti-Aids Clubs in schools. Members took a pledge to avoid vaginal sex until they were married. UNICEF AIDS experts that I consulted later in Harare seemed unimpressed with this approach. However they seemed to have little idea of alternatives that would be effective.

The condom issue has clouded many church initiatives. When working along the shore of Lake Kariba in 1987 some Catholic nuns consulted me about the women in their parish. They asked what they could do to protect themselves from being infected with HIV by their husbands when they came for a week-end after working in Lusaka. I advised condoms but realized that it might be difficult advice for the nuns to give. The condom issue came up later in Eastern Zambia when Theresa worked at St Francis Hospital from 1993 to 1995. I joined the AIDS Education team to talk in schools where we always had a PWA (person with AIDS) in our team. As we drove to a school I joked: "you can't teach condoms if you don't wear your seatbelt!" PWA's were always the most effective in convincing students that AIDS was real. They were also able to show how having several sexual partners increases one's chances of acquiring the virus. The Hospital made a useful contribution in collaboration with the local church by offering free HIV testing to those getting married. My main contribution on this and other occasions was to explain why mosquitoes do not transmit HIV and that there is no risk from sharing a toothbrush – but don't do it anyway for other reasons like colds!

Probably our first involvement with indigenous, separatist churches was when we lived in Serowe, a town in the north of what is now Botswana. We became friendly with a Zionist community that had been evicted from Rhodesia. They were a very cohesive and strong group. A slide show we gave, using some slides we were sent by Theresa's parents, of the Oberamagau Passion Play, made a great impression. They had a touching faith in the power of official documents and rubber stamps. Leaders who travelled were issued with a "passport" which said they were travelling on the "Lord's business" and should not be charged. They had an orderly village allocated to them outside Serowe and lived largely by making items of wooden furniture. Such groups could have been used much more to develop co-operative farms. When we lived in KwaZulu-Natal, South Africa in the 90's we were impressed with the Shembe people and their strong communities which hopefully help them to fight AIDS.

We were able to share some of our experiences with AIDS when we were asked to speak at a seminar of the Oxford Centre for Mission Studies (OCMS) in Oxford, UK. While we tried to show some of the problems that churches have had with AIDS we also spoke of the huge potential they have to contribute. Anne Bayley, a colleague in Zambia when she was Professor of Surgery, has written a challenging book for Christians – "One New Humanity".[11] The book attempts to answer the question "What can we do about AIDS?" She refers (page 282) to other faiths including African traditional religions.

My own church, the Quakers, have been concerned to help with Africa's AIDS crisis but have not known quite what to offer. When I was teaching at Prince Edward School Harare in 1991 I noticed boys in the library constantly huddled around one book. One day I looked over their shoulders and discovered to my surprise that it was a well illustrated medical textbook on AIDS. I found that the teacher, another Quaker, giving courses on AIDS, told any individuals not convinced by her teaching to look at the book. I mentioned this in an article in The Friend and almost immediately got an offer to send out 10 more. With a short questionnaire I discovered several boys had not believed AIDS was real until they saw this book. Several said they wanted their parents or girl friends to see it. It seemed a drastic approach but did it save some from being infected? A fellow Quaker who has made an important contribution to bringing AIDS under control is Glen Williams of Oxford. He has travelled all over Africa and other continents to produce a series of booklets – Strategies for Hope.

Quakers are accused at times by other churches of not being Christian. There is no doubt that a few would not call themselves Christians but none could deny the very deep Christian roots of the Society of Friends in Britain. Kenyan Quakers sometimes need to be reminded that the Society started life in Britain and only later extended to North America. Many Quaker yearly meetings in

Kenya and the USA are as evangelical and biblically based as the main stream churches. We have not allowed our wider view to stop us working alongside or interacting with other Christians and indeed those of other faiths. AIDS came into this when I approached a Christian bookshop in Empangeni, South Africa about St. Valentine's Day. This event is now commercialized, just like Christmas and the bookshop tried to counter attack with posters. I suggested that, like the Salvation Army, they should use the devil's techniques to put across a message of faithful, monogamous relationships. A study of St. Valentine's life shows that this is a perfectly valid message. A possible campaign along these lines, putting a small pamphlet into Valentine cards was rejected outright by the bookshop. In Harare, Zimbabwe, when getting Quakers accepted as contributors to religious broadcasting, there were objections from other churches which were fortunately thrown out on a technicality. Edna Caddick, a Bulawayo Quaker, became a popular broadcaster with a fan mail for her 0600 am broadcasts! When I suggested Muslims should have some airtime one minister said it would be over "his dead body".

One of the regrets of my time in Nigeria from 1954-8 was that I never managed to visit a unique Christian community. A colleague from Rural Education, Pat Walters, did manage to visit the Apostles of Aiyetoro and has sent me her notes. She describes "feeling as if we were returning from a voyage into the Old Testament". According to Mr. E.H. Duckworth, the Editor of the magazine, Nigeria[12] the community of 2000 (in 1951) was formed "with no Government, Mission or other outside assistance". He also describes it as "an earnest attempt to apply New Testament teaching to every day affairs". The reason I was unable to visit this inspiring community was difficulty of access. It was situated 104 miles east along the coast from Lagos. Access was through 30 miles of swamps and creeks from Okitipupa. Both Pat Walters and Mr. Duckworth travelled by government launch.

I have noted in several African countries communities similar to the Aiyetoro Apostles who live communally. They are usually characterized by strict discipline and in the case of Aiyetoro, when Pat Walters visited, no money was held by individuals. As Mr. Duckworth pointed out they provide "a form of organization that might equally well be applied to agricultural communities and these enable them to engage in large-scale modern farming methods". If Robert Mugabe's land handouts had been to organized Christian communities more food might have been produced than by his cronies. Similarly if the Ujamaa village policy of President Nyerere had involved cohesive groups like the Apostles it would have stood a better chance of succeeding.

As an agriculturalist and doctor, we have interacted with missionaries in many countries. The nearest we got to being on a missionary pay-roll was at Kaimosi Friends Africa Mission in Kenya from 1962-65. I was actually funded by the British Government and recruited by British Quaker, Roger Carter, when he was Principal of the Teacher Training College. We were given a doctors house next to the Hospital so that Theresa could easily get to the wards. The mission authorities pronounced that because we were now missionaries they could not pay her a salary. A compromise was eventually achieved by paying her 300 shillings a month to cover the cost of medical journals. My missionary contacts came in useful when working as a consultant in a number of countries. Often one is trying to obtain information as quickly as possible. The strategy I developed was to concentrate on government officials in the morning, commercial people in the afternoon and missionaries in the evening! The commercial people were the least likely to have a siesta after lunch! I have no objection, like another British teacher who was recruited through Friends House, London to being called a missionary. Indeed at one time, in 1989 we were both interviewed intensively by the United Society for the Propagation of the Gospel, for mission jobs in Zambia but were told they had no suitable posts. Later, when Theresa took a government funded post at St Francis Hospital, the Diocese of Bath & Wells raised £2000 to supplement her salary – but this was later diverted to support a mechanic.

The post-independence period in the 1960's proved to be full of hope for the future. I edited a book entitled "New Hope in Rural Africa"[13] which was based on a Conference held in Kikuyu, near Nairobi in September 1967. The contributors were largely agricultural missionaries and church workers while we from Makerere University in Uganda provided the organization. The preface to the book was provided by Trevor Huddleston who was then the Bishop of Masasi in Tanzania. He mentions an Easter card from his close friend President Julius Nyerere in which he quotes from the Acts of the Apostles: "No one claimed for his own use anything that he had, as everything they owned was held in common". This was what inspired the Arusha Declaration which launched the Ujamaa policy of consolidating peasants into villages. As we at Makerere were the Agricultural Faculty for the whole of East Africa some of us were asked to run a seminar on Ujamaa for the staff of the Tanzanian Ministry of Agriculture. Our reception was disturbing as officials seemed, with considerable justification, to find Ujamaa difficult to operate on a nation-wide basis. A researcher later claimed that the most successful Ujamaa village was the one operated by British American Tobacco! Close grouping of workers made sense for tobacco but not for widely scattered food crops.[14]

One of the papers at our Conference was given by the doyen of agricultural missionaries, Stephen Carr of the Church Mission Society (CMS). We have interacted with Stephen and his wife Anne in Kenya, Uganda and Zambia. My first knowledge of Stephen was when I shared a room with a missionary at a Rural Life Christian Conference who had found his tremendous faith and commitment too difficult to live with. Stephen is currently "retired" on a small farm near Zomba, Malawi and carries on his own extension work with soya beans, Vetiver grass and a range of innovations to help peasant farmers. His greatest achievement was in Uganda where he started the Nyakeshaka Tea and Strawberry Programme of school leaver settlement which survived the disruption of Idi Amin's and Milton Obote's regimes and continued to be highly productive. In 1967 he argued passionately for more agricultural training to be given "on the job" rather in the classroom. He pointed out very wisely that someone trained in a college with running water, electric light and toilets is unlikely to make a go of farming with a hut and hoe.[15]

Much of the hope propounded in the title of my book was short-lived. We set up the Christian Rural Fellowship of East Africa and were determined to keep in contact. I, as Publicity Secretary, was asked to organize our second conference in Entebbe Uganda. We were then overtaken by the Idi Amin coup of January 1971. East Africans were anxious about visiting Uganda so I had to find an alternative venue at Lugari, over the border in Kenya. The Fellowship continued for several years but with travel severely curtailed, particularly between Uganda and Tanzania, it was eventually wound up. At the Lugari gathering 80 plus members attended representing 8 nationalities and 9 denominations. They travelled from as far south as Songea in Tanzania and from Gitarama in Rwanda. Such disastrous losses of local enthusiasm for development, which have been undermined by politics and national rivalries, can be found all over Africa.

In 1998 Theresa and I attended a conference of Christian agricultural workers that seemed like a re-run of the gathering we held 30 years earlier. The inspiration came from a remarkable Kenyan, George Kinoti, Professor of Zoology and concerned Christian. His book "Hope for Africa and what the Christian can do"[16] shows "what every African, and especially the Christian, can do to bring dignity, justice, peace and material well being to this great continent". The drive behind the 1998 conference came very largely from Africans whereas in 1967 a high proportion were expatriates. It is a hopeful sign that Kenya managed a peaceful regime change with the election of December 2002. Richard Leakey, who has done so much for the country in different capacities, spoke enthusiastically on the BBC Radio 4 Station in February 2004 about the improvements to the economy, freedom of speech, etc. Hopefully Kenya will restore its economy in the way Uganda has done.

Other Christian involvements over the years have included:

1. Writing sections of "The Churches in Rural Development" for World Council of Churches, Geneva.

2. Consultancy for the Lutheran World Federation in Eastern Zambia (Lundazi) 1995.

3. Assistance with a brochure for the Church of the Province of Kenya – Eldoret, 1996.

4. Mission to El Geneina, West Darfur, Sudan for Quaker Peace Service, London to investigate problems with a project working amongst Chad refugees.

Trevor Huddleston's book "Naught for your comfort" helped to interest me in South African politics. When in 1958 I travelled for 4 months throughout Africa I contacted his mission. I arrived in Johannesburg by train from Beira via Rusape, Salisbury and Bulawayo. I still shudder at the thought of the young white woman in my carriage who produced a flick knife which she said was essential for anyone visiting Johannesburg. We later joined Gun-free South Africa when we moved to Mtunzini in KwaZulu-Natal in 1996. A Scottish surgeon colleague of Theresa's was shot by youths stealing his camping car not long after we arrived.

I was met at Johannesburg station by Father Jarrett Kerr of the Community of the Resurrection and stayed with the monks at Rosettenville. Courtesy of a relative in Anglo American, Howard Taylor, I had help with transport. I was taken for a visit to the offices of Drum to Jabavu in Soweto, named after the father of Noni Jabavu, then married to a relative, who I had just visited in Kampala. Another visit was to the Huddleston swimming pool in Alexandria Township. One day I spent in Sophiatown which was partly disman-tled on its way to becoming the white suburb known later as Triomphe. I ignored the warnings of the woman on the train and wandered around the township on my own to see the "We Wont Move!" signs and young men playing golf. Through my Anglo American contacts I was taken thousands of feet in a cage to see the miners sweating it out below sea level in a gold mine. But I was also able to insist on a visit to a miner's compound. Here I saw the congested, inhuman conditions which doubtless have now been improved. But the worst aspect of migratory labour was the sepa-ration from families and the disruption in family life which has contributed so drastically to the rapid spread of AIDS. In two years time I was to witness a miner's train off loading near Francistown in Bechuanaland. The miners, loaded with their purchases, were then flown from the airport to Angola, Congo and Tanganyika.

Later, in 1960, I organized the transport of a plane load of refugees from the Sharpeville Emergency in South Africa to the same airport. This was done with behind the scenes cooperation of the British authorities. The refugees were flown in a small plane from Swaziland to the Serowe bush air strip, accommodated for a few days and then driven overnight by lorry to Francistown airport. This was then under the control of the Witwatersrand Native Labour Association. Although they had been told not to interfere with the Ghana Airways DC3 I was warned to get off the field before take-off in case some of the South African staff objected to my involvement.[17]

A memorable refugee was Sam Kahn, a Jew and former sole Communist M.P. in the South African Parliament. He had been elected when the Constitution provided a very limited franchise for "qualified natives". Amongst the various religious groups who were involved in the South African struggle Jews shine through for their willingness to suffer for their convictions.[18] Another notable refugee was Oliver Tambo's wife Adelaide and two of her children. Although the organization of the airlift was done in London and Accra I once had to discuss some details with Oliver over the phone in Seretse Khama's house. Church groups in Serowe were helpful in providing accommodation for the 25 refugees and also assisted them in Swaziland.[19]

Reading the biography of Trevor Huddleston by Robin Denniston[20] one is surprised by some revelations about his life. For us, retired near the small town of Crickhowell in South Wales, we were surprised that he was Patron of Tools for Self Reliance which has its main Welsh workshop in the town. In 1991 he received its 250,000th tool at a ceremony in Sheffield (page 190). This was followed by a requiem for Fr. Martin Jarrett Kerr CR who had been my host in Sophiatown in 1958. Other revelations were his whipping of choir boys for getting drunk on communion wine (page 214). Another was that he was under treatment as a diabetic from 1955 to his death in 1998. I knew of his difficult old age but not that depression was a problem for much of his life. His biographer wrote that he "needed enemies as well as friends, anger as well as love to propel him into political protest" (page 40). In Tanzania he was "desperately tired" and felt "No one .... has any use for me except as a source of gifts – money, jobs, rides, footballs" (page 92).

Perhaps most surprising were his rages such as when after arriving in Mombasa in 1960, disgruntled from his experiences on 'The Warwick Castle', his consecration was postponed (page 86). Unlike Guy Clutton-Brock, who refused the retirement in Zimbabwe offer of Robert Mugabe, Huddleston wanted to die in South Africa – but failed. The major problem was that he needed 24 hour support but this could only be provided if he was in a nursing home. Since all white nursing homes depended on large numbers of black staff it smacked too much of the Apartheid years. He found life in a white old people's home "intolerable" (page 201). "He was not at all sure he wanted to go back or could face the political hassles of the new South Africa". What is certain is that Guy Clutton-Brock would have despaired of the "political hassles" if he had retired in Zimbabwe!

Retirement in Africa could be a good option for people from Europe because of the unlimited supply of labour to man nursing homes or to help in private homes. We were tempted but chose the home country option partly because of feeling responsibility for our small farm – but mainly to be near children and grand children. There are sometimes reproaches over employing servants, which no doubt Huddleston might have shared. We have always employed people on the principle that where there are large numbers of unemployed one has an obligation to employ people. Furthermore it is common in all African countries to employ servants and it was a well established practice from well before colonial rule.

In Nigeria as a bachelor I needed some help for the three months of rural travel I did in my pick-up. I stayed in bush rest houses where one carried ones bed, table, tin bath and chair plus cooking pots and food. Paul was an ex-Army batman and invaluable since I could leave my vehicle with him, start my visit to the school and return to a hot bath, made up bed and evening meal. Next day, while I was in the school, he would have the vehicle packed by midday ready to move on. In Eldoret, Kenya in 1995-6 our house had 2 servants quarters with toilet and shower so we were besieged with job and room hunters. One elderly Afrikaner lady, when asked why she had not moved with her family south, replied: "Why should I when I live in the most perfect climate in the world (at 7000 ft), have my garden I planted over 50 years ago and a wonderful cook and gardener"!

Most missionary societies expect their missionaries to return home at a fairly strict retirement age. Some, like Canon Hewitt at St Francis Hospital, Katete in Zambia manage to stay on into their eighties. In his case he was hospital chaplain but eventually left like Huddleston. Visitors in the 1980's were impressed by his memories of the first car entering Fort Jameson (Chipata) from Nyasaland (Malawi). He also walked there from the railhead at Broken Hill (Kabwe). A Friends African Mission nurse, Edith Ratcliff recently died in Kenya at the age of 85. She made a point of her wish to die in Kenya by buying a coffin which she covered and used as a coffee table! Kenyan Quakers gave her an impressive send-off with 13 hours of testimony over 3 days at the end of her 57 years of dedicated commitment to the church.

Africa, like most countries in the world, has benefited from the arrival of refugees, particularly from developed countries like Iran. We narrowly missed being in Persia for the coup which overthrew the Shah and converted it to Iran. We both had offers of prestigious posts in the town of Shiraz. Theresa was to be a Professor in the medical school and I was offered a post by UNESCO to advise on agricultural education. When 2 other offers came up in Zambia we took them mainly because we would not have to spend 2 years learning a language and alien culture. In Zambia we encountered refugees from the Iran coup, particularly from the Bahai Community who were severely persecuted by the new regime.

I had come across the Bahai faith by chance in Uganda in 1958 on my journey through Africa. To get from Kampala to Nairobi I took the train and found it to be full of Bahai's. They had just held a major gathering and had blessed a beautiful temple on the outskirts of Kampala. It was on our road to the University Farm, where we lived from 1966-72, and we once called to see it when they were worshipping. They warmly welcomed us, asked us to join them and invited us to share a passage from one of our religious books. They emphasize world peace in many of their sacred texts and we have always found them wonderful to work with. In Zambia I cooperated with a Bahai agriculturalist to cover the school they set up near Kabwe on the farming TV programme Lima Time.

Our attempts at working with other faiths and religions have been helped by the fact that we belong to a very small sect – the Quakers. In some places the nearest Quaker was a hundred or more miles away. In Mtunzini, South Africa we made the 1½ hour drive to Durban about once a month and joined in the local church on most of the remaining Sundays. The 9.00 am service was alternately Anglican and Methodist. In one group discussion on evangelism we were given a list of points when targeting someone for evangelism. I said "I'm your man!" but was assured by the minister: "You're a Quaker, you're different!"

During the Gulf War in 1991 we got to know the Iraq Ambassador to Zimbabwe. He almost overnight lost his tennis partners – the American and British ambassadors. We tried to fill the gap and within the Fellowship of Reconciliation helped to organize a demonstration in Unity Square after the war to minimize further violent responses – using a Pepsi-Cola banner. After some talks with Muslim leaders Theresa was presented with a Koran, inscribed by Musa Menk of the Council of Imams.

Desmond Tutu's remark that Africans feel they "have been brain washed" by missionaries probably applies more to South Africa than to East Africa. In Zululand there was the example of Bishop John William Colenso and his friend Theophilus Shepstone. They worked together in the 1850's to install "policies which recognized aspects of African culture, procedures and structures of power in a colonial situation".[21] They saw the need for the "recognition of the (Zulu) laws which ordered the homestead, patriarchal dominance, polygamy and, at a local level, the authority of the chiefly political order".[22] Colenso responded very positively to the questioning of his assistant in translation, William Ngidi. A recent example of the questioning of missionary intentions comes from East Africa. Ado Tiberondwa,[23] a Ugandan from Ankole makes the case for missionaries being agents of colonialism. The Kaimosi American Quaker missionaries would vigorously deny this although the education they provided was very similar to that provided by British missionaries. The greatest case for Desmond Tutu's remarks being representative of much wider African opinion is that so many African Christians have moved away from the mainline "missionary" churches.

Religion has played a major role in Africa since the dawn of time. The interventions of Christian and Muslim missionaries have overall had a positive effect. In our fifty years of involvement we have seen major contributions particularly in the fields of education and health. When a full history of the AIDS epidemic is written it may well show that Muslim Africa was able to withstand its onslaught better than Christian Africa. But, as with government, neither churches nor mosques have been able to keep up with a twenty year doubling of population. No country can cope with that sort of demand yet many religious bodies have failed to address the problem. Family planning facilities are still virtually non existent in rural areas. In Kenya the annual Catholic and Muslim bonfire of donated condoms in Nairobi was absurd both from the point of view of AIDS and family limitation.

NOTES

1. Aggrey of Africa by Edmin W Smith, Student Christian Movement, London 1929.
2. African Theology by Prof. Gabriel Setiloane, Skotville Publishers, Johannesburg.
3. p. 72 in "The Quaker Movement in Africa" by A.M.B. Rasmussen, I.B. Tauris, London, 1995.
4. Luhya is a term developed in the 1930's to describe closely related Bantu-speaking peoples including Bukusu, Tiriki, Kabras, Marachi, Maragoli, Dakho, Isukha, Kisa, Nyole and Samia – in the Western Province.
5. Age, Prayer and Politics in Tiriki, Kenya by Walter H. Sangree, London OUP 1966.
6. In an unconnected development in Zambia in the 1980's we were involved in a joint Quaker-Salvation Army project to revive the abandoned mission station at Ibwe Munyama, near Lake Kariba. Ginnie Goodfellow still lives on the lakeshore nearby on a horticultural holding.
7. Sunday Nation, Nairobi 10/12/95.
8. African Mythology by Geoffrey Parrinder, Paul Hamlyn Publishing, London, 1967, page 15.
9. The Ochre People by Noni Jabavu. John Murray, London, 1963, page 24.
10. Author of Godly Medicine, Shona Religion and The Shona Witch. He lived from 1912-1985.
11. One New Humanity by Anne Bayley, Society for Promoting Christian Knowledge, London, 1996.
12. Nigeria No. 36 1951 published by the Government of Nigeria and available free on payment of one shilling and six pence to cover postage.
13. New Hope for Rural Africa, Editor E.R. Watts, East African Publishing House, Nairobi, 1969.
14. Joan Wicken, Nyerere's Personal Assistant and companion, died aged 79 on the 5th December 2004 after 50 years dedicated service to Tanzania. She was an attendee at a Yorkshire Quaker Meeting after retiring to the U.K.
15. Since this chapter was written Stephen Carr has published his autobiography – "Surprised by Laughter". The Memoir Club, Stanhope, Weardale, Co. Durham. 2004.
16. Hope for Africa by George Kinoti, International Bible Society and AISRED, Nairobi, 1994.

17. Later involvement with South African politics and a meeting with President Kaunda, accompanying Hendrik van der Merwe, are covered in another chapter.
18. Father Jarrett Kerr told me that much of his support in Sophiatown came from the Jews. Later,in the 1970's and 1980's I got to know Abe Galaun in Lusaka. He had escaped from repression of the Jews in Lithuania during the 1930's and built up a thriving, hides butchery and farming business in Zambia. He once stopped me in Cairo Road and asked if I could find a good use for surplus money in one of his trust funds! When talking to my students he made fun out of his decision to call his champion Hereford bull, Karl Marx!
19. R. Watts, Memoirs of the Refugee Pipeline. Botswana Notes & Records Vol. 29.
20. Trevor Huddleston, A Life by Robin Denniston, Macmillan, 1999.
21. The View across the river by Jeff Guy, David Philip, Claremont, 7708, South Africa. 2001.
22. As 21 above.
23. Missionary teachers as agents of colonialism by Ado K. Tiberondwa, Kenneth Kaunda Foundation, Lusaka, Zambia, 1978.

CHAPTER IV

The Transition to Independence and Beyond

LOOKING BACK OVER the 50 years since 1954 a major mistake by the British governments of the time was the policy of accelerating the granting of full self government. In Western Nigeria internal self government was granted in 1957 ahead of full independence which was given on 1st October 1960. The Princess Royal, assisted by the Governor, Sir John Rankin officiated and Chief Obafemi Awolowo took over internal affairs as Premier of the Western Region. We colonial recruits were offered new contracts and could retire or transfer to other regions or even the trusteeship of Cameroon. When I offered my servant a day's holiday to celebrate self government he replied that he had nothing to celebrate because, as I was being Nigerianised, he would soon lose his job! There were always losers as well as winners during moves to independence.

The point about the period between internal self government and full independence was that Britain retained major responsibilities. It also meant that Britain handled foreign affairs and the army and retained some financial responsibility. The massive cost, for a small country, of setting up a complete diplomatic service, including embassies, could be delayed until full independence. Expenditure on prestige items like Mercedes Benz, executive jets, regular shopping trips to London, would be delayed. The expensive tastes of some African rulers and particularly their wives have been a cost many countries could have done without. An example was the very small country Swaziland. Recently[1] King Mswati demanded £8 million be spent on palaces for his 10 wives and 2 fianceés. Previous luxury items have included fleets of cars and aircraft.

When I boarded the M.V. Accra, of the Elder Dempster line, in the docks at Liverpool on July 29th 1954 I did not realize the significance of the date. It was later fixed as the last date for Western Nigeria expatriates to qualify for compensation due to loss of a life-time career in Her Majesty's Colonial Service. I had been recruited in 1953 as a Rural Education Officer and had spent a year acquiring a Post-graduate Certificate in Education. The year had been spent in London in the tropical areas section of the Institute of Education in Senate House. One day a week I crossed the road to learn Hausa in the School of African and Oriental Studies (SOAS).

I eventually accepted the lump sum compensation, known in the service as "Lumpers" rather than the small pension or transfer to another colony. The idea was to use part of it to explore the other British, French, Belgian and Portuguese territories of Africa and then return home. My twin tasks then were to study more economics at Oxford University and find a wife who shared my interest and concern for Africa. Agricultural postings in Africa often involved living in remote areas and I felt the need for a companion. In 4 years service I had witnessed several marriages torn to breaking point by the boredom of wives and incompatibility. In particular, if an expatriate wife had no substantial role, she often declined into a life of bridge and sundowner parties followed by depression and alcoholism. To find a lifetime partner during a 3 month leave who shared my interests and had the qualifications to work in Africa was too ambitious. In practice it took from April 1958 to July 1959 for me to find and get to know my future wife Dr. Theresa Piper, propose and get married. We first met at London Yearly Meeting in Friends House, Euston in 1958 when we both spoke during a session on Africa and had a coffee afterwards. Our marriage took place at Jordans Friends Meeting House near London on 18th July. My best man was Ronald Weldon, a medical student while we both had African friends as guests – Victor Ngu of Cameroon, Alhad Hatimi and Barudi Nabwera from Kenya.

The rapid movement of Nigeria towards independence became obvious on board the M.V. Accra in August 1954. In the First Class we had the "Sardauna of Sokoto, one of the leaders of the north and apparently due to become Prime Minister under the new

Constitution" (Letter home "off Gambia" 7/8/54). "Although he dresses in very stately robes he is a very pleasant man to talk to and he has given me some of his papers to read". These were from the Constitutional Conference he had just attended in London as leader of the main party in the north, The Northern People's Congress (NPC). He was also known as Sir Ahmadu Bello and was one of the politicians murdered on 15 January 1966 during the Ibo led officers' coup. The leader of the coup was Major Ironsi who I saw in 1956 sitting in the front seat of the Queen's Rolls Royce when she came to Moor Plantation, Ibadan. He was appointed ADC for the royal visit. Ironsi was himself killed by northern troops in July 1966 and that uprising was followed by a massacre of Ibo's in August and September. From 30 May 1967 to 12 January 1970 the country was torn apart by the Biafra rebellion which was eventually defeated under General Gawon. He was in turn overthrown during an Organisation of African Unity (OAU) meeting in Uganda. He had the presence of mind to quote Shakespeare – "'All the world's a stage and all the men and women merely players. They have their exits and their entrances':[2] This is my exit!"

Over the past 50 years African leaders have not been noted for graceful withdrawals from power. General Gawon's conversion from state president to student at Warwick University was a remarkable one. Other graceful withdrawals have included those by Kenneth Kaunda and Julius Nyerere. In Kaunda's case he handed over after a questionable defeat in an election. Arap Moi in Kenya handed over after a peaceful election but only after several previous violent election campaigns involving dubious tactics. When we moved to Moi University, Eldoret in 1995 for Theresa to teach in the Medical School we were advised: "Come after one election and leave before the next and you will have a peaceful stay!" It is easy to take a negative view of democracy in these circumstances but fortunately Kenya persisted. The December 2002 Election was relatively peaceful. Moi once said in reference to Zaire in 1997: "It is Africans themselves who are causing chaos under the cover of democracy".

On board the M.V. Accra in 1954 I had an old associate from Reading University, Roy Manley. "By living a more or less free lance life on board and not getting involved in any one group Roy and I have got to know quite a number of interesting people. Last night I chatted for over an hour with Chief Arthur Prest, Federal Minister of Communications. He has had a very varied career and only 6 or so years ago was studying law in London. Like most African politicians he believes that most Europeans deliberately misrepresent conditions in Africa. Our films, papers, etc. he claimed all show the African as still a savage". (Letter home from off Gold Coast 11/8/54.) After 50 years Africa still often gets a rather negative coverage in the Western media.

I went on to compare the Sardauna and Chief Arthur Prest. I should mention that a young northerner, a son of the Emir of Kano was very helpful to us. In the case of the Sardauna I missed out on an invitation to visit to his home in Bauchi when my posting was changed to Ibadan. The letter went on: "As the 2 Ministers on board are from different regions it is interesting to see their attitude to one another. On the surface they treat each other very civilly but from what they say (to us) one can tell that they are really at loggerheads. It looks very much as if Nigeria is going to become another India with a Northern Muslim country and a Southern, mainly Christian country. Such a split would probably be disastrous economically" (Letter 11th August 1954).

Chief Arthur Prest lost his ministerial post not long after I arrived. When I was on tour in his town of Warri next April I was able to call. "He was living in a small flat upstairs" over "a Café-cum-Pub" with the rest of the house let out. "Unfortunately when I arrived about 5.00 he was still having a nap and by the way he was shouting at his servants must have been rather upset at being disturbed. However he seemed quite pleased to see me and we chatted for an hour or so. The main topic of conversation was 'Primitive Art'! He took the line that there was no point in collecting and preserving relics of Nigeria's past. Like many African politicians he feels that they may be used as evidence of African backwardness. I tried to point out that at present Nigerians are too near to the time when idols were worshipped and that in a 100 years or so such relics would be valuable to the country". We went on to discuss current political developments and he had been mentioned as a possible Western Region representative in London (letter dated 4th April 1955).

My wife, then Theresa Piper, went to Uganda in 1956-57 to do her pre-registration year prior to being a fully qualified medical practitioner. As a single woman she was invited to parties at the Kabaka's palace and Government House where Sir Andrew Cohen was Governor. Alan Forward, who spent his colonial career in Uganda, documents how internal self government worked in his case.[3] "Mr. J.T. Simpson, the Chairman of the Uganda Development Corporation, is the Minister of Economic Affairs, an appointment designed undoubtedly to reassure the commercial community and foreign investors". Most of the collapsed economies in Africa have suffered from poor financial management and a failure to raise taxation to meet the financial needs of ambitious plans for better health, education and roads. The old balance between increasing exports to pay for more imports was often neglected. In many cases the deficit was made up by adding to national debt.

After I left the Colonial Service in 1958, with my lump sum compensation for loss of career, I wrote feature articles for the *Daily Times* in Lagos. The first was entitled "Future of Nigerian Agriculture" (Nov 24 1958). I had experienced in my work as Rural Education Officer that "most educated Nigerians tend to look down on the farmer whose labour has contributed very largely to their progress". "Ask a group of school children how many intend to become farmers and you will be laughed at". Yet, I pointed out "virtually all the exports" which pay for "the importation of manufactured goods" are "agricultural products like cocoa, palm oil and ground nuts".

My articles did not mention oil exports which in 1958 were in their infancy. Exports of traditional commodities such as cocoa were £N131.8 million while crude oil exports were £N1 million, representing 0.8% of total domestic exports.[4] By 1966 oil exports accounted for 33% and soon were dominating the entire economy. As I feared, agriculture declined, urban drift increased and unemployment became more and more widespread. Much of the income from oil went to the western companies that developed it. As in so many countries farmers were paid a miserable percentage of what their crops were earning overseas with the balance going to government or corruption. The debt crisis in African countries has this other side to the one which is most emphasized in the liberal western press. Too much debt was accumulated after independence for projects which had no chance of generating funds to repay the debt.

The lenders bear an even greater responsibility than the governments because they employed highly experienced economists. In a consultancy I did in 1989 for the International Fund for Agricultural Development (IFAD) in Rome I learnt at first hand how profligate these agencies could be. I was disturbed by the consultant who flew in for a few days and prescribed a million pounds worth of computers for a rural development programme. As with most international aid organizations I was unimpressed by the displays in their palatial building that tried to show their concentration on poverty. I was particularly upset by the lack of concern in IFAD and amongst my fellow consultants over the fact that no family planning facilities were available in this densely populated area of Cameroon. A recent (2003) report shows Cameroon have the poorest availability of family planning facilities out of 31 developing countries.

IFAD was formed in the 1970's and was used to mop up surplus US dollars from the surge in oil prices forced by the Oil Producing Exporting Countries (OPEC). It followed the pattern of the World Bank and other multi-nationals with long-term loans for agricultural, infrastructure or industrial projects. Very few of these were ever likely to generate sufficient income to pay off the loans. One of the more successful organizations which bridged the transition gap was the Commonwealth Development Corporation (CDC). It was formed in 1954 and learnt from the disastrous lessons of the Tanganyika Groundnuts Scheme. This was launched in 1947, well before independence, to meet a predicted shortage of vegetable oils. Largely due to poor planning and a failure to predict droughts it was a disaster. There was an overdependence on mechanization. We visited the remains of the 3.5 m acre Kongwa Groundnut Scheme in 1965. Over lunch we were able to share the enormous Kongwa Club facilities – full-size billiard table, large swimming pool and several tennis courts – with the 3 remaining members – one African, one Asian and one European! Some of the CDC post-independence schemes pioneered investment in small-holder coffee, tea and sugar. These avoid socially unacceptable labour lines and in Kenya some have produced tea of high quality.

There must have been considerable confusion over the speed of handover at various levels of colonial administration. John Smith CBE was recruited in 1950 as a Colonial Cadet and attended one of what were called Devonshire Courses before being posted to Northern Nigeria. He relates in his memoirs an interview he had, soon after arrival, with the Governor. "I recall that, asked by the Governor how long a career I thought lay before me, I replied: 'A certain five years, a probable ten, and a lucky fifteen'. I was told, 'You have 30 years or more ahead of you. My own son is coming into the service next year'."[5] From this it is clear that British policy changed rather suddenly to a "have full independence tomorrow" policy.

My experience and that of John Smith's are two indications of the lack of a long-term approach to the hand over of the colonies. Jack Straw, the British Foreign Secretary, recently blamed "many world problems" in Africa and Asia on Britain's post-war policies.[6] There is certainly truth in his assertion but I would put at the top of the list the unnecessary speed of transition to full independence. The interim period of regional self government in Western Nigeria, although also too hurried, was a positive period in Nigeria's history. The fact that Portugal hung on to what was in effect colonial rule until 1975 in spite of American pressure to grant independence shows that Britain could have lengthened the transition process to 25 or 30 years.

Africanisation, or the replacement of expatriate staff by nationals, often followed full independence quite quickly. In my case it came well before full independence. It was delayed in some countries, such as Zambia and Malawi, by British funding of schemes like OSAS (Overseas Service Aid Scheme) and BESS, which helped to keep British staff in universities. The pace of what was also called indigenisation varied considerably from country to country. I was Nigerianised, in that I handed over to a Nigerian Agricultural Officer. I still have a copy of The Nigeria Handbook inscribed on 16th December 1957: "Presented ... by the entire staff of the Agricultural Station, Fashola, Oyo, Nigeria as a token of love and affection on the occasion of his departure from Nigeria on leave and retirement". It was signed by those in charge of the office staff, the field staff and the engineering staff. I had only been in Nigeria for 3 years and 3½ months.

I do not think that my friend in Ghana, Kofi, knew that the effect of rapid full self- government would lead to an exodus of people like me. Government people understood we had been given an ultimatum to give up our career prospects. I had a tougher time with the Student Christian Movement executive committee. I had been serving the SCM as their Senior Friend Secretary. "They seemed very upset at my going. However I explained that I wasn't leaving because of self-government and they seemed to some extent reassured" (Letter of 23rd October 1957). My most high profile hand over was in Zambia where I handed over the television programme, Lima Time, which I had presented for 3 years, to Enock Sikapande – on television. I wrapped up the red floppy hat that had become my trade mark and presented it to him in a studio programme.

The most dramatic transition from colonial rule to independence took place in the Portuguese territories of Guinea, Mozambique and Angola. This followed the successful coup against the dictatorship of President Antonio Salazar in Lisbon on 25 April 1974. I had made 2 visits to Angola – first as a traveller and second as part of a team of consultants. It was a friendly, beautiful and diverse country with a tremendous potential. While attending the 1973 agricultural show in Nova Lisboa (now Huambo) I had lunch with a Rhodesian farmer. He was very confident of the future of the country because he said race relations were so much better than in Rhodesia. He had flown his Hereford cattle, combine harvesters and tractors in a C130 plane. Within months he must have lost everything as the country fell apart. I did not warn him of an impending catastrophe and indeed my only memory of cracks in the regime was when I talked to Portuguese national service recruits who were very unhappy. While working along the border with South West Africa (Namibia) my Cuanhama mixed race interpreter took me to meet his Portuguese sister. It soon became obvious that his father had 2 wives – but they seemed to make a very well integrated "rainbow" family. Urban schools seemed to be totally mixed and integrated under the assimilation policy.

In 1958 I visited French Cameroon, the French territory of Middle Congo, the Belgian Congo and then crossed Africa by rail, boat and bus from Lobito in Angola to Mombasa in Kenya. There was little sign of impending independence in any of these countries. A week in the Belgian Copperbelt at Kolwezi gave an impression that much had been done to train Africans as technicians but not as managers. All the senior mine staff I met were Belgian.

In 1975 I had a brief one man consultancy with the United Nations looking at the Young Farmers of Uganda and developing an aid package. For weeks I had problems with the authorities sparked by a rivalry between 2 senior officials. Spending hours in then Kampala International Hotel I developed an Egyptian friend amongst the OAU Angola independence negotiaters. Idi Amin was then President of the OAU. Reports I got from my Egyptian friend, when we had breakfast together, were depressing. There seemed no prospect of an amicable solution with 3 liberation movements fighting for power and the cold war was still at its height with the USA and USSR supporting different sides. In retrospect it is surprising to be reminded that Savimbi was supported by Zambia for several months after the meeting. On an Aeroflot stop-over in Luanda, the capital of Angola, in 1979 I met Nathan Shamuyarira of Zimbabwe who was later for many years one of President Mugabe's ministers. After gazing at the refuse scattered around the airport he commented: "Even if you have had a revolution you can surely afford some brooms"!

As a newly appointed Colonial Civil Servant in the 1950's one did not expect to have much contact with senior Nigerians. In retrospect it was amazing how many Nigerians one met – including politicians. Chris Groves, a CMS missionary at St. Anne's School, Ibadan invited a wide range of people to play on the school tennis courts. There I met Anthony Enaharo, Minister of Home Affairs, later famous for being a political prisoner in Nigeria under both the British and Nigerian administrations. His biography reveals his liking for the British in spite of his being imprisoned in Brixton prison pending extradition to stand trial for treason. It also reveals that he abandoned tennis for golf after going to the tennis racket section of Simpson's in Piccadilly. The "sports professional", who challenged him to play golf instead of tennis, offered "three free lessons and if I liked the game I should pay for another nine".[7] He never looked back and didn't bother to get a new tennis racket!

Tennis featured in a political incident I was involved in at the Oyo Tennis Club in May 1957. It was at the time of an election prior to the granting of self government to the Western Region. There was great rivalry between the main parties – the Action

Group and the National Council of Nigeria and the Cameroons, the NCNC. The NCNC probably stole the net as we became identified with the Action Group, the ruling party. There was a religious aspect as the NCNC were mainly Muslim while the Action Group were mainly Christian. Some well off Christian schools had tennis courts but there were none in Muslim schools.

In my letter home dated 20th May 1957 I wrote:-

"Our club net in Oyo was stolen" recently during "a reception for the Alafin, the big Chief of Oyo. He was largely chosen on political motives and so it was assumed that our club supported the government party. The rival party thereupon decided to teach us a lesson by pinching the net! The committee are now trying to get the government to buy a new net!"

The sequel was that the government refused and instead we had a special reception graced by the Alafin. Margaret Taylor, a recently arrived CMS missionary learning Yoruba, and I had to play an "exhibition match" before a small crowd. Tragically the books at the end of the day didn't even balance let alone show a profit towards a new net!

We have found sport clubs a good way of socializing and meeting a wide range of people on neutral ground. However after we married in 1959 and moved to Kaimosi in Kenya in January 1962, we soon ran into the last vestiges of Apartheid in that part of Africa. We joined the Nyanza Club in Kisumu where many of the missionaries went to swim at the weekend. One day we took a fostered baby, who later became our adopted daughter Kageha, to the club. She was too small and weak to swim and was lying on a towel. The Secretary came out and demanded that she be removed. We protested that she was part of our family. The quick retort came: "That madam is your problem"! On a visit to the Club in 2004 I looked up its history. There had been a long battle to change the rule that "only British subjects of pure European descent" ... "would be eligible for election as members". The first Indian, Mr. Khosla was elected in March 1963 and the first African member, Mr. Onyango, was only elected in 1967. Compromise measures to allow a wider use of facilities for golf and tennis started in the 1950's. The Information Department supplied 2 copies of the Prime Minister's portrait in November 1963 and the committee decided to balance these with 2 pictures of the Queen. The 2004 membership seemed to be mainly Asian but there were plenty of African members and local schools were allowed to use the pool.

It was during the period after Kenyan Independence on 12 December 1963 that some fairly drastic steps were taken by politicians. Jomo Kenyatta had been elected Prime Minister following the June 1963 election. The ruling party the Kenya African National Union (KANU) a year after independence converted Kenyatta to be President and the country to a republic. However, a leading Luo with left wing tendencies was made Vice-President.[8] This was Oginga Odinga, who was considered by some of the Kaimosi missionaries to be almost a communist.

I had known Barudi Nabwera, one of Odinga's local supporters, in Britain when I was on a Quaker international work camp in London and he later attended our wedding in 1959. The work camp was incidentally led by a Colonial Service agriculturalist from Kenya, Donald Thomas. I was in charge of arranging Sunday evening speakers in the college so it was natural for me to invite a leading local politician with a Quaker background. I was criticized for inviting Barudi to speak. He later in the 1980's was made Party Secretary of KANU and, like most politicians in that position, became unpopular.

Oginga Odinga was not re-elected to the office of Vice President in March 1966. However, in 1965, when I was the newly appointed Principal of the Embu Institute of Agriculture, I had a distant encounter with him. I received a phone call from the Embu government office to advise me that he was passing the college in less than half an hour. All students were to line the route and I had to run around all the class rooms to pass on the instruction. The students were sluggish in their response but fortunately it took longer than expected for him to arrive. He walked in front of his Mercedes up the tree-lined avenue from the town wearing "Ahero" sandals. These were made in the Nyanza markets from old tyres and were his way of identifying with the poor. It might also have shamed some of his colleagues who were already living a more luxurious lifestyle and enjoying the fruits of independence. He was a flamboyant but caring man. He would have hated being called in Kiswahili a "Wa-benzi" – those who ride in Mercedes Benz cars.

My appointment as Principal in Embu is, I think, the only post I obtained on what might be called "the old boy net". We had been attending the Nairobi Agricultural Show in 1964 when I bumped into Paul Mirie, a fellow Reading University student, who had recently been appointed Director of Agriculture. Kenyanisation was rapid for top level posts. He said they urgently needed someone to fill the vacancy for Principal and was asked whether I was interested. Ian Wallace, who by chance changed places when I moved to Makerere University, Uganda, in 1966 was Principal at Embu and later at a similar institute at Bukura for several years. Kenya gave a greater emphasis to agricultural training than most other countries and took steps to keep expatriates in key positions.

My post at Makerere University, Uganda was a joint UNICEF funded appointment, for part of my 6 years there, with Philip Mbithi, a Kenyan sociologist. He, partly unwittingly, got very involved in high Kenyan politics in the 1990's. In between he had become Vice-Chancellor of Nairobi University and was later made Head of the Public Service and Secretary to the Cabinet. For a few days in March 1996 he did an unthinkable thing – he refused to take up a Presidential appointment. He had been told by President Moi to become the first Kenyan representative in the revived East African Community. His refusal produced headlines and concerns for his safety as well as "deplorable" statements from Moi supporters. When the press went to interview him at his Machakos ranch he was said to have disappeared over the horizon on a tractor!

One of the common characteristics in the early days of independence in virtually all countries was the concentration of power in the hands of a small clique. When this happens in countries like Britain and the USA vigorous criticism is usually allowed. Wahome Mutaki in the *Daily Nation* (7 March 1996) wrote of Mbithi "he wasted himself by making it impossible for a government led by another party to employ him". "He has left a legacy of an intimidated Civil Service". He left, however, with a reputation for being his own man and an ability to withstand bullying. On a visit in 1998 we called without warning at his ranch and received a warm welcome.

It would be fair to claim that no country has been able to maintain the standards of the civil service they inherited at independence. Probably Botswana has been the most successful. On the other hand civil servants in a society where they have many close relatives with dire needs for health, education and business expenses are under unbearable pressures. The extended family is still a strong and largely positive phenomenon throughout Africa.

Makerere in the 1960's was at the cross roads of East Africa. Our Faculty of Agriculture equally served Uganda, Tanyanyika and Kenya.[9] The Kenyan Minister of Education, Jeremiah Nyagah, who we had got to know well in Embu (his constituency), once interrupted a lecture to greet me. He was invited to tell the students what he was doing in Uganda. He was one of a relatively small number of politicians to retire with a record of continuous dedicated service to his country. On Sundays he would often take a service for my students and was a devout Christian. Politicians like him made some of Kenyatta's cabinets rather special in comparison with other countries. Exceptional politicians included Tom Mboya, Robert Ouko and Mwai Kibaki, who was elected President of Kenya in December 2002.

Jeremiah Nyagah was one of the main speakers at the funeral of Carey Francis, former head of Alliance Boys High School, outside Nairobi. He died soon after independence in 1966 and tributes to his influence on political life in Kenya were impressive. Oginga Odinga[10] in the Foreword of Francis's biography wrote that of all the "British colonial personnel – missionaries, civil servants, settlers …. Carey Francis was one of the very few whom I admired and respected even though I did not accept all that he stood for". He admitted Carey Francis "had a soft spot for him" and had been "a source of inspiration to me during all the ups and downs of my political life". He was partly responsible for making Kenya's first politicians stand out for their abilities compared with the rest of Africa.

Tributes to a man who had a remarkable influence on Kenyan politics came from a wide range of people. One of the 6000 that walked for his burial at the school was asked why he was special. He replied: 'Because he was on our side'. I committed a blunder in 1963 when I saw a man under a tree at a garden party in the Alliance Girls High School. My opening gambit was to ask: "Are you connected with Education?" The Rev. Stanley Booth-Clibborn, later Bishop of Manchester, was then Editor of the Christian Council newspaper. He wrote that I had committed the biggest gaff of the year. "Carey Francis was Education in Kenya!" – as head of the leading school where around half the cabinet were educated and later as an inspector and policy maker he had immense influence on Kenya's first years of independence. Obviously many other educationalists played important roles. Education has for many years been taken very seriously by Kenyans through the Harambee schools, village polytechnics and intense local fund raising. In the days when Luo's were finding it difficult to get jobs at home we met many teaching outside Kenya. We once joked that the Nyanza Province must have more PhD's per village than any other part of Africa!

Another important bridge between aid giving countries and Africa is through education. If this can include contact with people in their homes there is a much greater impact and understanding for both parties. We recently received an ecstatic thank you from a Tanzanian computer student at Swansea University. He said a day spent helping with the annual shearing of sheep on our hill farm was his best day in Britain. The autobiographies of Africans like the late Joshua Nkomo confirm the major influence of visits overseas beyond the particular training they had come for. Miss G.O. Chiepe, who for several years was Foreign Minister of Botswana, spent part of her study time in Bristol living in the home of Roger Wilson, Professor of Education and a Quaker. Another Quaker, Ruth Gillett of Bromsgrove, wrote to give me an introduction to Chief Obafemi Awolowo when he had recently become Prime Minister of Western Nigeria. I wrote home on the 16th July 1955:- "I went to see him at his private house, which is quite near the centre of the town. It is a very unpretentious place for a P.M. to live in and very different from the ordinary run of Minister's houses"... "You go down a sort of alley way and climb up a narrow staircase." He used to go to the Friends International Centre, when a student in London, and was invited by the Gilletts to spend Christmas with them. "He remembered all the children's names" and the places they had taken him to. He impressed me by his simple life style and commitment to the future of his people. The severe reductions in the numbers of Africans getting scholarships to study in western countries is regrettable and will drastically reduce such contacts. The fact that African students not on scholarships pay substantially higher fees in British universities than local students is to be deplored.

Theresa, when a pre-registration doctor at Mulago Hospital, Kampala received reverse hospitality. She was invited to stay with Dr. Julius Gikonyo Kiano and his American wife outside Nairobi in 1956. She knew him through various joint Makerere friends. We met him at another post-independence Nairobi Agricultural Show when he was Minister of Commerce and Industry. He flung his arms around her as a long lost friend and then asked us to look after several of his children while he went for an urgent meeting. About this time he became momentarily unpopular when he divorced his American wife and got her expelled minus her children.

Chief Obafemi Awolowo was probably one of the most committed of African politicians. He was said to have created "one of the best run political parties in Africa".[11] The 1973 *Who's Who* described him as an entirely self-made man", "brought up by Protestant missionaries and still a non-smoking teetotaller". "His eternal problem has been to win national support". While his missionary education obviously influenced him in becoming a teetotaler it may also have contributed to his perennial problem of getting on with the Muslim North. In the December 1959 election he fought on a national basis but ended up as a leader of the opposition. He was involved in a party split which ended in fighting and his eventual imprisonment, along with Anthony Enharo, on a charge of treasonable felony. He was released early by General Gowon in 1966 who said "we need you for the wealth of your experience".

David Williams, a Briton, who was Editor of the widely read magazine *West Africa* from 1949 to the 1980's knew Awo, as he was called, intimately. He once drove him to visit Dame Margery Perham, biographer of Lord Lugard and authority on Nigerian history, in her Berkshire cottage. In a personal memoir after his death [12] he recalled his sense of humour when campaigning for the former German colony of Northern Cameroons to join Nigeria. The political message made little impact until an official said the main "choice was between the French and the English. So Awolowo found himself campaigning, and successfully, he told me with a wide grin, for 'the English'". David Williams made a major contribution to what unity exists between West Africans – at least the ones who read English!

In 1951, as Secretary of the Reading University International Society, I was asked to find a speaker to tell us about the Gold Coast and Nationalism. This was because it was expected to be the first British colony in Africa to get independence. I wrote to what was then a British official, Mr. Leach, The Commissioner for the Gold Coast. He declined, as he said he couldn't discuss political issues, but recommended David Williams. We did not take up Mr. Leach's offer to talk on marketing boards but in retrospect we may have been unwise. The takeover of cocoa advice, grading and marketing, from companies like Cadbury's and Mars, was politicized and within years the independent Ghana lost its place as the main supplier of cocoa to the world. Fair trade for Africa's farmers is in 2004 a very live issue but an extremely complicated one.

The Gold Coast was the first country where I had an African friend – a pen friend. He used the address on a letter I had written to the magazine *Picture Post* in 1949 when I was doing my National Service as a conscientious objector on a dairy farm. He was 17 and had a confusing number of different names. I will use Kofi. Kofi told me of the imprisonment of their leader Kwame Nkrumah. To be what was afterwards called a PG or prison graduate enhanced a politician's reputation in those days. Some extracts indicate Kofi was totally in favour of rapid independence:- letter of 10.3.1950: "The British Government came to civilize us and we are now civilized. Why shouldn't they leave the Government of the country to us. We are therefore demanding our rights and freedom". "Half of the population is unlettered and all is due to the Government we have over here". Letter 1.5.1950 "There is no colour bar in this country". "The whites and the blacks who are having high posts in government have been given bungalows built at quiet places of the large towns. We are fighting for our political emancipation. Some of our leaders have been imprisoned because they organized a country-wide strike. Let us hope that we shall get our Full Dominion Status in the near future". Other letters mention "our great national leader, Kwame Nkrumah" who was in prison.

Nkrumah was released on February 12 1951 to become Prime Minister and picked his ministers under a limited form of self-government. On March 6 1957 Ghana became the first colonial African state to get independence. When I visited Accra later that year I stayed at the prestigious newly built university at Legon and

55

was taken to see the Independence Monument. John Hargreaves, who taught history at Fourah Bay College in Sierra Leone used a picture of Kwame Nkrumah lighting "the perpetual flame of African freedom" for the cover of a study he wrote.[13] He wrote under the heading "The Sudden Death of West African Colonialism":-

"Although the political acceleration was inaugurated under the Attlee government it did not become politically controversial; Its principal strategist appears to have been Andrew Cohen of the Colonial Office – following his return from Uganda".

While some "acceleration" was needed the main aim of the nationalists was, it seemed to me, internal self government rather than full independence.

On a recent (2003) visit to Zimbabwe we found a once thriving economy in tatters. This was after 20 years of reasonable progress under majority rule. My friend Kofi in Ghana must have been disappointed with how, after their majority rule, the economy severely declined. However Ghana has in recent years made reasonable progress. The cry all over Africa is for stable economies, more jobs and an end to crippling inflation. Could a slower process of granting independence have achieved this? Perhaps Botswana gives some clues to how Africa could have been managed.

Our experience of Botswana was well before independence when it was the Bechuanaland Protectorate. This had meant little alienation of land as in Rhodesia and South Africa. John Wilde, a British High Commissioner in the late 1990's, gave a talk on the theme: "Botswana: Africa is working".[14] He showed what dramatic economic progress has been made since Independence was achieved on September 30 1966. The fact that it has maintained its momentum, unlike many other countries, can be attributed to the fact that there are no deep tribal divisions. Seretse Khama, the first President, avoided one party rule by having regular elections but in practice he and his party the Botswana Democratic Party has held on to power.

Key elements in Botswana's success have been the discovery of massive diamond reserves which, fortunately, Cecil Rhodes didn't know about. The diamond industry has been run to maximize benefits to the country unlike oil in so many other countries. But a key element has been what is in effect one party rule by consensus.

Elections in Zimbabwe have turned out to be destructive of the economy because they have been used to divide the country along tribal and racial lines.

Once full independence was achieved expatriates had a limited role at elections, mainly as observers. My main involvement was in 1954 in Western Nigeria. 2 months after my arrival I was put in sole charge of an election in a village school at Olodo, 10 miles out of Ibadan. The Headmaster and 4 teachers assisted but there were no police to keep order. The main problem was that before someone voted the electoral roll had to be checked. This consisted of 20 A4 sheets and most names were not in alphabetical order. A high proportion of names started with A so it could take 30 minutes to check one person.

"By mid morning we had a large crowd trying to get in the building with the candidates agents holding the doors to stop a flood. My instructions said "Ring Ibadan" if you need help. However there was no phone so when I found there was a nearby railway station I sent a telegram through the station master. It read "SEND ONE OR TWO POLICEMEN AS SOON AS POSSIBLE". They arrived in about an hour and all was saved. One slight crisis was when an illiterate voter didn't appreciate the slot for his voting slip and forced open the seal! It was with great relief that I handed in my boxes at the Town Hall.

The main parties in the election were represented by symbols for the benefit of illiterate voters. Slogans such as "COCK (NCNC)[15] STANDS FOR CHAOS" and "Vote for Palm Tree and Prosperity". The Palm Tree represented the Action Group and the symbols were put on the boxes minus the slogans. I saw one school compound covered with leaflets torn into shreds – presumably because the teacher supported the other party.

Democracy has not worked well in most African countries but it is far from perfect in other parts of the world. For a neutral comment on a visit to Zimbabwe in 2003 we said "we don't like our leader either but we don't know how to get rid of him"! Democracy has had its ups and downs all over the world. Africa must persist and the fact that Zambia, Malawi and Kenya have all replaced governments through elections in recent years is a hopeful sign. To quote Inge: "Democracy is a form of government which may be rationally defended, not as being good, but as being less bad than any other".[16]

The biography of Daniel arap Moi,[17] formerly President of Kenya from 1978 to 2002, supplies some interesting details of the interactions between the Leakey Family and Kenyan politicians. The father of Charles Njonjo was houseboy to the late Dr. Louis Leakey before independence. We interacted with Louis' first son, Colin Leakey, when we lived next door to him and his family at the University Farm in Uganda. In the early 1980's when lecturing to students at the University of the Transkei I was asked by a black student: "Could a white be elected president of an African state under majority rule?" I replied that it was unlikely but, in view of the recent election of Philip Leakey in a 99% black constituency to the Kenyan Parliament, it was not impossible. When we lived in Eldoret, while Theresa taught at Moi University from 1995-96, we experienced the reactions to Richard Leakey's support for the opposition Safina Party. The Moi Government's nervous reactions seemed to be out of all proportion to the numbers in the Safina party – mainly because of Richard's leadership.

During the early years of independence several African regimes relied heavily on expatriate or white settler advisers or administrators. During a tour to lecture in 1988 on majority rule for the Institute of International Affairs I shared a taxi to Johannesburg airport with a Malawian businessman. He told me that President Banda had just appointed a number of white administrators to take over defective para-statals in Malawi. Attending a university conference at Amsha in the 1970's I shared a room with a Swedish professor who was chief adviser on economics to President Nyerere. President Kaunda in the 1970's seemed to be surrounded by expatriate advisers. When James Oglethrope, who came to Zambia originally as a Dutch Reformed missionary, retired from State House to South Africa, President Kaunda hosted a farewell event and made a gracious speech in spite of the fact that he was then providing the African National Congress with its main base in Africa.

One of the least likely governments to rely on expatriate advisers was that of President Obote in Uganda. Yet in 1969-70 the Dean of the Faculty of Agriculture at Makerere University was asked to submit a confidential report on the activities of the Ministry of Agriculture. As a lecturer and Faculty Liaison Officer I was asked to contribute to the report. We already had a fairly frosty relationship at the University Farm because we were in a Kiganda area of opposition to the government. The Dean was funded by the Rockefeller Foundation and many of his staff were British or American. While it was clear that the Ministry of Agriculture was very ineffective, in what should have been a crucial role for developing Uganda, we were in no position to correct that situation. The Permanent Secretary had a reputation for being negative about any proposals from his staff and little could be done while he was there. This is one reason why, in the first 15 months of Idi Amin's rule things looked more promising. I was even commissioned to organize a workshop on the air freighting of fruit, vegetables and flowers in March 1972. Within weeks every available aeroplane was involved in the exodus of Asians following Idi's "dream" that he should expel all 80,000.

In conclusion I would say that the transition to independence and democratic rule was mishandled by both the colonial governments and the new indigenous administrations. Too little effort was put into keeping the services of crucial expatriate personnel. Inexperienced local staff were appointed for ridiculously short periods. In the case of the Lima Time TV presenter he was sent to the USA within weeks of taking over. Expatriate advisers were too often appointed on political grounds rather than on technical and African experience.

NOTES

1. *Times* 14 Jan 2004.
2. As You Like It Act 2 scene 7.
3. "You have been allocated Uganda, Letters from a District Officer" by Alan Forward. Poyntington Publishing Co. 1999, page 127 DT9 4LF.
4. L.H. Schatzl, Petroleum in Nigeria. Oxford University Press for NISER, Ibadan 1969.
5. John Smith. Colonial Cadet. Duke University Press. 1968 page 6
6. See debate in *The Times* 19 Nov 2002. London.
7. Fugitive Offender: An autobiography. Chief Antony Enaharo, Cassell & Co., London, 1965, p. 142.
8. Politics in Ex-British Africa by J.F. Maitland Jones. Weidenfeld and Nicolson, London, 1973, page 54.

9. It was common to have a class made up of 11 from each country with 3 out of the 11 being Asian.

10. Carey Francis of Kenya by L.B. Greaves, Rex Collings, London, 1969.

11. Who's Who in Africa by John Dickie and Alan Rake, African Buyer & Trader, London, 1973, page 322.

12. West Africa, London, May 18 1987.

13. The End of Colonial Rule in West Africa by John Hargreaves. The Historical Association, London, 1976.

14. Royal African Society, Bristol Branch Meeting, 9th Feb 2004.

15. NCNC stands for National Council of Nigeria and the Cameroons.

16. William Ralph Inge "Our Present Discontents" Outspoken Essays, First Series, 1919.

17. Andrew Morton "Moi: the making of an African Statesman", Michael O'Mara Books, London, 1998.

CHAPTER V

Africa and the Media

AFRICA HAS BEEN covered in the last hundred years with a gradually increasing media attention – through the press, through radio, television and with a seemingly endless series of new devices. The press was becoming a powerful influence in Britain and North America during the 1800's and particularly from the Crimean War onwards. James Gordon Bennett's conversation with Henry Morton Stanley on 28 October 1869 was an early sign of the power of the western press and its potential interest in Africa. When Stanley complained that finding Livingstone would be expensive he replied:- "Draw a £1000 now; and when you have gone through that, draw another thousand, and when that is spent draw another ….. and so on, but find Livingstone".[1] We are not told whether Bennett was rewarded sufficiently with increased circulation for his expenditure!

We came across an early example of the power of the press when we lived in KwaZulu-Natal, South Africa in 1996-9. We were in the area where the Anglo Zulu War was fought in 1879 and one afternoon investigated nearby Fort Napoleon and the deserted station with the same name. The Prince Imperial of France was exiled in Britain and his mother used her influence to get him some war experience. When he was speared by a Zulu in a skirmish there was an outpouring of grief, embarrassment and recrimination not unlike that which followed the death of Princess Diana. In his few weeks in the country he had become a popular figure in Natal society and the media made sure this popularity spread to Britain.

The Prince Imperial story was strung out over weeks and months partly because the body had to be taken by horse carriage, train and then on HMS Boadicea to England for burial. The press in South Africa and Britain made a meal of the incident. There were issues of precedence if he had been buried in Westminster Abbey. As in the case of Princess Diana the press had to find someone to blame. There was even scope for conspiracy theories. It came at a time when the Anglican Church was divided after Bishop Colenso decided that Zulu objections to some of the Bible stories they had been told were valid. With the massive defeat of the British Army at Isandlwana it led to Disraeli's classic remark: "A remarkable people the Zulu: they convert our bishops, they defeat our generals and they have written finis to a European dynasty"![2] Today's media would have had a field day. It was remarkable that, as far back as 1880, the Zulu's had some sympathisers amongst the British press. This may have contributed to the return of King Cetshwayo to Zululand on 10 January 1883 at Port Durnford – near where we lived from 1996-9.

With the coming of the Boer War at the end of the century the press were able to fill pages with blow by blow accounts. Winston Churchill made his name as a Morning Pest journalist by getting arrested, detained and then by staging a spectacular escape over the wall of the prison and through the streets of Pretoria. It was such a dramatic story that today it would have justified an entire page with quotes from his family and his background. Instead the *Daily Mail* of December 28th 1899 gave him a single column of about 12 inches. The news was straight and less digested in those days. On the same page there were nearly 30 other items and the *Daily Mail* had Boer War correspondents in Colenso, Gibraltar, Cape Town, Bombay, Modder River, Sydney, Wellington, Mafeking, Tuli, Mochudi, Naauwpoort, and Pietermaritzburg. This was impressive coverage of what was going on. It was however noticeable that there was almost no mention of the effects of the war on the African population. Today Africa is rarely covered in most papers and then the story is usually of a disaster of some sort. The emphasis for both TV and print journalism is on the good photo opportunity as a back up to aid organisation advertising.

When we were on leave from Uganda in 1968 we purchased a derelict hill farm in the Swansea Valley as a safe haven in case of coups, etc. By chance, soon afterwards, while we were still in Uganda Richard Attenborough made the film "Young Winston".

The scene of the arrest of Churchill during the Boer War when a train was blown up was filmed within sight of our farm which appears for about 10 seconds in the distance. We took it as an indication that some parts of the Transvaal look a little like Welsh moorland. Our little station at Penwyllt Quarry was renamed Chieveley for the filming.

Nowadays films are not such a critical part of the media impact on Africa. It was in Uganda under Obote in 1970 that the British Council lent me a 16 mm copy of Animal Farm to show to a very mixed open air audience of students, labourers, children and local farmers at the University Farm. Although in English, which many did not understand well, the audience got the message very quickly. Under President Obote the government was intensely disliked by the Baganda peasant farmers who surrounded the farm. During the 4½ years prior to Idi's coup in 1971 we failed to get any ministers to attend our functions when invited. When one minister visited us unannounced a gun dropped out of his pocket when he bent down to tie his shoe lace. The Animal Farm film had a message of what life is like under a dictatorial police state which is easy to recognise.

My journalism really started with "Letters to the Editor" when I was working on farms as a conscientious objector from 1948-50. Winter evenings were fairly tedious when living on inevitably remote Welsh sheep farms. Letters went to local papers and one to the *Picture Post* produced a response from the Gold Coast. In the Colonial Service journalism was not encouraged but later I enrolled for 10 lessons with the London School of Journalism. While at St Peters Hall, Oxford from 1958-59, studying for a Diploma in Agricultural Economics, I wrote a series of features for the *Daily Times* of Lagos on Agriculture in Nigeria. I despaired of "the apathy of educated people towards agriculture" (Nov 24 1958).

When I was half way through my 10 lessons in journalism we were travelling by sea from Venice to Mombasa in 1964. We had a re-fuelling stop at Aden – then a British territory – late in the evening. To escape the heat on board we took a walk up the main shopping street – a hive of activity late in the evening. Returning to the boat with our 3 year old daughter I saw part of a local newspaper, floating in the breeze, – and stuffed it into a pocket. It proved to contain an article in English on the island of Socotra as an alternative British base if it was retained after Aden's independence. Trying out my new journalism skills I found an encyclopedia and wrote it up as a feature for the *East African Standard* in Nairobi. It was published and produced a string of letters from ex-military men who had been there in the war. I re-wrote the article, incorporating the additional information and sent it to the *Guardian* – where it was published! Incidentally Socotra was not retained as a base. Sadly I have had few opportunities, for this "background gathering" technique!

It was in Wales that I had my first lucky break into free lance journalism. We had left Uganda very peacefully by train to Mombasa and then on the Lloyd Triestino MV Africa in April 1972 to Tenerife and later London. There were already murmurings about the Asian Community and indeed President Obote had driven most of them out of their village stores in the 1960's. By chance, as Agricultural Correspondent of the *Uganda Argus*, I had an article pointing out their contribution to farming on the same day as President Idi Amin's first public attack on them early in 1972. About the same time the small community of Israeli's were expelled. By the time of his dream that all Asians should leave within 3 months we were safely in Wales.

My involvement in media work and journalism was a natural progression from my Makerere post in Uganda. I was a UNICEF funded Lecturer in Agricultural Extension – which covers all aspects of getting information to farmers. The subject includes the use of all available media. As time went on I tended to widen my field from a focus on nutrition to cover rural technologies such as water and sanitation, solar and wind power, HIV and AIDS plus Quaker concerns related to world peace. I never aspired to a full-time career in this field and was happy to write for local African newspapers. My most useful and rewarding assignment was to produce an agricultural feature every month for the Central Office of Information (COI) in London. It went to British embassies and high commissions in Africa and would sometimes appear in several papers and magazines. With a good stock of reference materials from West and East Africa I was able to write wherever I was – in Africa or Wales. When we moved to Zambia in 1977 I was already known in the Commercial Farmers Bureau because they had been using the features. One of the best parts of the agreement was that

I could submit 2 or 3 black and white photos with each feature. I could call at any High Commission in Africa and get beautiful enlargements of my photos.[3] Regrettably I was axed in a Thatcher economy drive after 10 years.

For a short period correspondents were allowed into Uganda after Idi Amin's coup. However they were gradually expelled in 1973 and only one BBC reporter remained. His reports invariably came on at 0800 am on the BBC Home Service and that news was too late for the papers. I eventually was able to give the background to the latest news in the *Guardian's* foreign pages. Our son was then at primary school on the border of the farm and had to be collected at 0330 pm. A routine developed where I phoned the Guardian Foreign Desk about 0900 am and got clearance for a story of a certain length. I then had 4 hours to contact people and research the subject. At 0200 pm I would phone the *Guardian* and dictate my piece over the phone. I was ready by 0330 pm to collect our son from school. A reader of the *Guardian* objected to this practice but did not realize that any article without a byline has been written in the paper's offices and not by a foreign correspondent. A bizarre situation arose when I discovered the Foreign Editor was a bee-keeper. In between my assignments on one occasion we discussed how he would move his bees to London when the *Guardian* moved from Manchester! London's parks provided excellent bee fodder when the workers flew out of a tube in the Editor's flat!

A good example of the difficulties facing journalists in times of crisis occurred when I was in a BBC World Service studio in Bush House, London. In Uganda Charles Harrison, for whom I had written when he was Editor of the *Uganda Argus*, was at one end of the line. There had been some shooting and troop movements in the streets of Kampala. The interviewer kept asking him to describe what he had seen himself. In the end it was clear that Charles's account was almost entirely based on a press statement by the Government!

In 1975 I was recruited by the Food and Agriculture Organisation to go to Uganda as a consultant. There had been a slight lull in Uganda's descent into chaos while Idi took the Chair of the OAU. My mission was to investigate the Young Farmers Movement and, if appropriate, develop an aid package. My

Guardian work was as a free lance journalist and I was never on the pay roll nor had I been a member of the National Union of Journalists. The problems I had, which eventually forced me to leave prematurely, were more likely due to internal rivalries and struggles. I did however gather what information I could for future articles. This had to be done very carefully. My main worry was that I could implicate Ugandan friends. As regards my own safety I was reassured to be given a UN passport.

Most of my accessible friends were at Makerere University and some lived on the campus. I could walk or catch a bus there. If I got lifts I was careful to walk the last stretch to the hotel because of the security men at the door. One friend, Sarah Ntiro, was then a senior administrator in the university. She insisted on dropping me at the door after a long chat in her house. In the middle of a detailed confirmation of the terrible goings on in State House over the past 2 years the phone rang. It was from State House and she was urgently needed by the President to interpret for a French speaking visitor. She later left the country and for several years lived in Nairobi. I was able to visit her in 1996 and she was well settled in Kampala with one son.

On arrival from Rome I reported to the headquarters of the Ministry of Agriculture in Entebbe. The Permanent Secretary was a Mr. Kunya who I had known well when I was at Makerere from 1966-72. He was very welcoming and we drew up an itinerary and programme of people to meet. The government was to provide a vehicle and driver. It was agreed I would start after the week-end when I planned to attend the Nairobi Agricultural Show.

When I returned to Entebbe on the Monday plane all hell let loose. I walked to the office of the Acting Permanent Secretary (P.S.) since Mr. Kunya had left the country on a course. My transport arrangements were cancelled and I was told to go to the Kampala International Hotel and await instructions. I have no evidence to believe that my writing for *The Guardian* had anything to do with this abrupt response. It was more likely that Mr. Kunya, being a Muganda, did not get on with the Acting P.S. who was a northerner. The reason he gave was that my papers were not in order.

Having worked 6 years in the country, been on the radio every week as presenter of a 30 minute farming programme, I was well known and had many contacts.[4] Other UN staff and consultants helped me to get around by providing lifts when they were travelling somewhere relevant to my mission. It was a cause dear to my heart, having been a member of Young Farmers Clubs in Brecon and Henley-on-Thames. As consultancies go it was ideal. I was a one-man show. The target group was limited and no large bureaucracy was involved. I was soon convinced that in spite of a breakdown in so many government activities there were still clubs operating with almost no support. A little help would have gone a long way. Basic gardening tools, seeds and fertilizers would have been key elements to my plan. I bitterly regret that it did not come off as at the time I was convinced that it was worth the obvious risks.

After several weeks of "suspension" by the Acting Permanent Secretary I felt I had enough information to write my report. I approached the head of the United Nations office and they consulted the Ministry of Foreign Affairs. They replied that as far as they were concerned "Mr. Watts was no longer in Uganda". If he was they suggested the UN should do something about it! I booked a flight and reported to FAO in Rome and was given time to write my report in Wales. The report was accepted by the Government of Uganda in 1976 but by then relations were deteriorating and the proposed aid never reached the Young Farmers. On a return visit in 1996 I heard that both the Permanent Secretary and the Director of Agriculture were dead. The first from natural causes and the second after a long period in prison where he died after being found as a living skeleton.

Both men had died in the 1980's when there was extensive fighting and unrest. I don't think the incident was related to my writing for *The Guardian* which would not have got to Uganda. The most likely explanation for my being declared a "non persona" is that once a query had been raised there was a chance it could be referred to cabinet. The "non persona" solution avoided that embarrassment for all concerned. There was in fact, at that time, the reverse of the usual struggle for top jobs. When I went to the Namulonge Research Station outside Kampala the sole concern of the Director was to get out of the country. A promotion to headquarters was very dangerous, was his implication. Anyone who watched when television cameras filmed one of Idi's cabinet meetings will remember the terrified faces of some of his ministers.

While very terrible things happened under Idi Amin it is a mistake for the media to always demonize dictators. Amin came from a very small minority tribe and was very vulnerable to rivals in the army. It meant that power gradually concentrated in a clique. Having met Idi for 15 minutes on the 3 small-holdings I researched on at the University Farm I had a sneaking respect for him. He was partly responsible for my getting involved in radio broadcasting. When he took over in January 1972 he not only put civil servants in charge of most ministries but also announced a major increase in radio programmes for farmers. This was announced at a "Farmers Forum" attended by farmers from all over Uganda. He said "as from next Monday there will be 30 minutes a day for farmers on Radio Uganda". Although his motives were mainly political, to gain some grass roots support, this emphasis on farmers was fully justified. Too often agriculture was neglected by governments after independence. An emphasis on media which reaches farmers is fully justified in all African countries.

After his speech the Chairman asked for names. Someone shouted my name, although I had slipped out of the hall. As the Liaison Officer of the Faculty of Agriculture I was allocated 30 minutes per week on an English programme entitled "Calling Farmers". The 30 minutes a day was not too difficult to achieve as we had around 20 languages to cover. The 30 minutes in English included a weather forecast and report, news items, research reports and a 10-15 minute panel with questions from listeners. I had been in the same class at Reading University with Anthony Parkin, later agricultural story writer of the BBC radio programme *The Archers*. A *Ugandan Archers* was considered but rejected as too difficult with our resources. There is however now (2004) a well established Ki-Swahili version broadcast from Nairobi with some British help in setting it up.

In a sense Idi Amin ruled by radio. The farmers for the Farm Forum which launched "Calling Farmers" were invited on the radio. A district officer had to listen to the early morning news in case he was summoning them for a meeting 100 miles away. My colleague, Professsor William Banage, heard he was appointed Minister of Animal Industry on the radio when he woke to hear the morning news.[5] This use of radio to control a country applied all over Africa. We visited Kenya for a Quaker Triennial Conference in 1982 at the time of the attempted coup against President Arap Moi. The main battle took place around the studios of the Kenya Broadcasting Corporation. At such times, as we learnt in 1972 with Idi's coup, the best thing was to lie low until it was clear what was happening. In Uganda we spent the day of the coup at a nearby swimming pool with our radios. In up country Kenya a remote community started celebrating prematurely in 1982 and several arrests were made – the coup had failed after a few hours.

In the case of the Idi Amin coup the first impressions were rather promising for both the Baganda and the expatriate community. Civil servants or university staff were appointed ministers, elections were promised and there was initially relatively little violence. A plan for an external service for Radio Uganda (RU) was announced within a month of the coup. It was to be provided by Philips Telecommunications and funded by the Dutch Government. When I was confined in the International Hotel in 1975 I had plenty of time to use my small radio. The South African Broadcasting Corporation (SABC) had the clearest transmission in English and Swahili. OAU delegates were forced to listen to it as RU did not carry news of the OAU Angola negotiations. Other news came from the BBC and the Voice of America.

In view of his later reputation, which was partly the result of media coverage and books such as the one by David Martin, it is unpopular to say something positive about Idi Amin. His calling of a Farmers Forum soon after his coup in 1971 and the announce-ment of a radio service for farmers of 210 hours per week was a stroke of genius. Radio is still the medium of choice for reaching farmers mainly because the print media is, in most countries, restricted to towns. Only Uganda, when the vernacular weekly paper *Munno* was distributed through the Catholic Church network, managed significant coverage of farmers. No doubt Amin's objective was mainly political. There is however a great need for Africa's farmers to get organized in unions and co-operatives. Marketing is the key to the expansion of food and export crops. When we lived from 1993-95 in Eastern Zambia, 500 kms on a terribly pot-holed road from Lusaka this point was driven into us. Returning from Malawi we found our former house help in Lusaka

(1977-82) on the road-side with a pile of maize bags. The only way he was able to get a reasonable price for what he had grown was to hitch-hike on a passing lorry to Lusaka.

We arrived in Zambia in 1977 when the war with Rhodesia was escalating. For one terrible period in 1978 we had a nightly black out from 0800 pm onwards. Eventually, because people found it difficult, the lights were switched off over the whole of Lusaka except the hospital. No one ever explained why the Rhodesian Air Force wouldn't drop bombs between dusk and 0800 pm! However it made a radio an essential item of equipment for evening entertainment. Fortunately the Rhodesian Broadcasting Corporation obliged with regular British comedies such as "Take it from Here". These weren't intended for us but for the Rhodesian forces on the border!

We have always been great fans of the BBC World Service and its broadcasts to Africa. Few people realise that it broadcasts in 43 languages including many in Africa. They have enhanced the reputation of Britain in Africa more even than the British Council which also provides an excellent library service. Thanks to the BBC, when we lived at the University Farm, Kabonyolo, we were the first to hear of the Idi Amin coup and warned parents that there would probably be no school that day. When we called at various houses parents were sending out their children to catch the school bus. We spent the day at Namulonge Club swimming and playing tennis with a radio handy. While in Zimbabwe on the 30th June 1990 we were at The Most High Hotel in Kariba overnight waiting to cross into Zambia when we heard that a coup had been staged by some elements in the army. The BBC correspondent had heard a 0400 am report on Zambian Radio News. The news was repeated on the 0500 and 0600 BBC World Service news but later denied as all the plotters had been arrested. By then however we had decided not to risk our visit to Lusaka. If only the BBC correspondent had been a bit more of an insomniac we would probably have made our visit! Travellers in Africa should be warned to carry a small, battery powered radio and tune in regularly to the BBC and local stations.

My most thankful memory of having a small radio in a tight situation was when I was staying in El Geneina Airport in the Darfur region of Sudan. The Rest House was in effect a deserted building and was only being used because there were a handful of pilots

70

from the Desert Locust Aerial Spraying Team camping there. There was no electricity or other form of lighting and I had no torch. 12 hours of darkness must have been what our ancestors lived with but is very difficult to adjust to in the twenty first century. Terry Waite, The Archbishop of Canterbury's envoy, once acknowledged that the BBC helped him pull through his incarceration in Beirut "more than God". Their radio was on almost 24 hours a day.

Involvement with the BBC Africa Service developed when we were based in Wales from 1972-77. Being on the Africa Committee of Quaker Peace and Service in Friends House, Euston Road, I was able to develop a pattern of recording interviews on recent African visits at Bush House, Aldwych around midday. A short bus ride got me to Euston for the committee meeting in the afternoon. There was no need to claim my rail fare from Neath because the BBC covered it.

My most memorable contribution to the World Service was to do the 5 minute comment which used to go out after the World News. After buying a news paper, on Cardiff station, I had a hunch that a Ugandan news item would make a good subject for a comment. I wrote what I had in mind by hand on the way to Paddington. On arrival I phoned Bush House and asked for the Newsroom Editor. He said come on in and phoned reception to get me a pass. He read my notes and then pointed to a typewriter. One would assume, at a delicate time, it would have to go to the Foreign Office for checking. But, after re-reading, the Editor sent me straight to a recording studio. The only evidence I have that it went out was my cheque and a phone call next day from an insomniac friend in Wiltshire who heard it at 0300 am! I am still irritated by the fact that in Wales we have been deprived of the World Service for so long. Even now it is only received if you have a satellite dish or on Radio 4 during the night and up to 0530 am. Radio Wales, which we can now get, gives us a 30 minute extension to 0600!

Further radio involvement came in Zimbabwe when in 1991 the Harare Quakers decided to get involved in religious broadcasting. This was organized through the Council of Churches. There were some objections that we weren't sufficiently hard core Christians! Exclamations of horror resulted when it was queried why the ZBC had no religious broadcasts by Muslims or Hindus. In the end it was discovered we were involved in the Council of

Churches from its earliest days. I was sent for a FEBA[6] training course in radio broadcasting. We were then allocated a few 30 minute slots and several 5 minute "Thought for the Day" type programmes. A Quaker in Bulawayo, Edna Caddick, developed a fan mail for some of her early morning broadcasts and kept them going for over 10 years.

My major media involvement took place in Zambia from 1982-86 when I was appointed Research Extension Liaison Officer at the Central Research Station at Mount Makulu. I continued with press features and for a time was agricultural correspondent for *The Times of Zambia*. Radio was well covered in the Ministry of Agriculture where they had their own recording studio. I could just submit a list of researchers who had appropriate messages on new varieties, disease problems or advice on fertilizers and liming.

My major media involvement in Zambia was in television. I had never liked the medium and indeed in the 1970's resisted our children's requests for a set on our Welsh farm. We eventually got a shop to test a TV at the farm and they failed to get anything like a picture due to the circle of mountains around our valley. We were relieved but succumbed in 1986 when the local village had organized a special reflector for our valley. We never owned a television in Africa and still have admiration for President Banda who resisted having it in Malawi for many years. I still feel that, particularly in Africa, television could have been introduced more communally to hold people together and to be more of an educational than an entertainment medium. Certainly the case for agricultural programmes is strong in a country where 90% of the population were born in the countryside. Even though Zambia is more urbanised than many countries the future depends to a large extent on agriculture.

Moving into my new job in Zambia I found there was nothing on farming on the television. One day I called at the studios and pointed this out. They told me to come back and try to produce something. An enthusiastic producer, Alfred Kalonga, was eventually assigned to me. I was called Researcher/Presenter so I had the freedom to find suitable topics. My boss in the Ministry of Agriculture – the Assistant Director for Research, Dr. Chibasa, was consulted and gave full approval. He also said "as long as the programme is giving the department a positive image don't consult me on what you cover". I agreed to spend not more than one day per week on researching and filming each 30 minute programme.

These instructions assumed some importance when we had been running the weekly programme for a year or more. The topic I chose, which had always been on my mind, was family planning! We entitled it: "Does a Zambian farmer today need a large family?" I started the programme with a visit to a mobile family planning clinic. For the last 20 minutes we returned to the studio for a discussion amongst Zambian researchers led by a geography lecturer at the university. On going to the Ministry next day I was called to the Research Office. Dr. Chibasa had left and been replaced by a M/S Robina Chungu. She was my last principal when I taught at the Natural Resources Development College outside Lusaka. I had already fallen out with her over not vacating my house quickly enough. She now rounded on me and accused me of embarrassing her and taking a delicate subject without permission. My response was to quote Dr. Chiluba's words and I thought the matter was closed.

Several weeks later I received a letter from the Director of Agriculture. It read: "The Party and its Government" request that the Lima Time programme should continue and receive all possible assistance. There was no mention of the family planning issue but reading between the lines I assumed that M/S Chungu had complained at a high level and the complaint was referred to the Cabinet or the President directly. "The Party and its Government" was Zambian civil service speak for "the President, Cabinet or Party".

It was a good example of how even in a one party dictatorship decisions can be made which incorporate different viewpoints.

Africa's presidents do not have "a good press" in the West and even President Kaunda was severely criticized. We have never seen any evidence of the millions salted away that he was once accused of in *Time*. He seemed to be a most abstemious man to us. In one case involving the media we found him very responsive. We had heard a report of a speech he made which stated that no one in Zambia should plant maize within a certain radius of their house. In effect this was a presidential decree which received world-wide publicity. This was because of a report that mosquitoes were breeding in maize plants. Theresa had recently done a survey of maize plants with an entomologist. Mosquitoes were certainly resting on maize but they found no evidence of breeding. On our way to Quaker meeting next Sunday we handed in her report at State House. Next day, when she got to her office in the University Teaching Hospital, the phone rang and it was the President. He thanked her and agreed to countermand the order after a cabinet meeting. Unfortunately, while the original order got transmitted world-wide on the BBC, the Voice of America, etc. the countermand was only heard on Zambian programmes!

The Producer, Alfred Kalonga, made several very important contributions to the programme. I knew nothing about the technical side and in fact usually didn't even see a programme until we went to our neighbours to see it on the night. Alfred soon had a feel for the programme and found a catchy Tonga tune to go with the credits. Alfred's background from farming stock in Southern Province was a major asset. The launch on September 17th 1983 had some preliminary hiccups when the Minister of Agriculture insisted on having 10 questions for his introductory interview and came with notes. He came well lubricated for the recording in the afternoon and I was heavily criticized for arranging it for after lunch. We had to do a re-take with a prepared speech!

Towards the end of my time a Dutch photographer in our Ministry, Werner Haas, cooperated with us, using his personal VHS camera. It meant we could be more ambitious in getting around the country. A previous series of recordings had to be cancelled as we were leaving the studios when the camera was taken to cover the unexpected arrival of the President of Burundi. The furthest we went was to within the sound of gunshots on the Angola border to make a series on the Limpopo Valley. I returned to Zambia with him in 1987 to make a commissioned video for a charity called Harvest Help covering their Gwembe Valley Project on Lake Kariba.[7]

From 1990-93 we lived in Harare, Zimbabwe and I tried very hard to get into television work again. We produced about 10 programmes but we never got the momentum or presidential support we had had in Zambia. Zimbabwe always seemed to have a much bigger overlay of resentment and suspicion than Zambia. It is amazing in retrospect that the breakdown that took place in the late 1990's didn't take place earlier. One of the aims of the programmes was to cover both black and white farmers and to increase national understanding of their contribution to the economy. In an effort to inform commercial farmers about the land reform I had been involved with in Kenya and Zambia I offered to speak to branches of the Commercial Farmers Union. The offer was taken up in Chegutu, Inyanga, Darwendale and Raffingora but I never managed to convince them that there was any urgency about the land issue in Zimbabwe. Some claimed the pressure was off due to the Economic Structural Adjustment Programme (ESAP).

Readers may well query why television programmes on farming should be stressed in African countries. As already mentioned radio is well developed in many countries and is by far the most effective way of reaching farmers. Television has more of a national role in educating political leaders, the rapidly expanding urban populations and above all those with money. The future for African countries without lucrative oil reserves like Nigeria or diamonds like Botswana, lies in agriculture. I bitterly regret now that my programmes on Zimbabwean TV did not take off as in Zambia. They could have helped to heal the racial rift over land ownership which now has wrecked Zimbabwean Agriculture. Fortunately some of the evicted commercial farmers are being welcomed in Zambia, Mozambique, Angola and even Nigeria.

The aspect of the media we have not dwelt on is that of the Western press, radio and television coverage of Africa. Returning to our Welsh farm in 1999 we found the African coverage minimal and invariably negative. One had the feeling it was driven by the large aid organisations such as UNICEF, OXFAM, Save the Children, CAFOD, Christian Aid, UN Food Programme, etc. While many African countries are not covered at all a crisis like that in West Darfur, Sudan receives pages with large photographs of dying people, rudimentary huts made from bushes and vehicles stuck in mud. There are daily repetitions of TV news items of dreadful camp conditions, with no hope of relief, for months. Nothing is said about the fact that the area has been in turmoil intermittently since the 1970's. Some of the media has attempted to whip up feelings over the raids on villages to have a major Western military intervention including economic sanctions. It seems the lessons of the Iraq invasion of 2003 have not been learnt by much of the media or by Tony Blair. Just a single mention of Western intervention in the media would have set back moves to get a large African Unity (AU) peace keeping force in place. Africa's huge problems of borders and inter-tribal violence cannot be solved by Western intervention except where it backs up local initiatives.

At the beginning of the chapter I gave a list of where 12 *Daily Mail (London)* correspondents were reporting from during the Boer War in 1899. One has the impression that nowadays newspapers do not have such widespread coverage. In the case of Darfur correspondents seemed totally dependent on charity bodies such as OXFAM and the Red Cross for their information and possibly travel arrangements. It was obvious that the Sudan government had massive problems of administering an area the size of France with almost no all weather roads. Few made any attempt to explain the complex tribal make up. When I worked there briefly in 1988 I learnt from the 1987 Baseline Survey that:

> The original inhabitants of the Darfur Region were non-Arab and sedentary but with "some elements" practicing nomadism. The Fur were just one out of 7 main tribes in this group but "with many small tribes" in addition. The Arabs in the region were originally traders or refugees from the destruction of the Christian kingdom of Dongola in the fourteenth century. In addition there were 15 Arab camel-owning or semi nomadic tribes and several tribes that have moved from Chad or other West African countries. These are all spread over an area the size of France with no all weather roads.

Reports from Sudan in the British media during August 2004 gave very little idea of the complexity of the situation in Darfur. When I was sent to the border with Chad in September 1988 the town of El Geneina was completely cut off by floods for days. The Quaker team there were working with refugees from Chad not local villagers. It seems clear there has always been uncontrolled two-way movement across this border. A fact that I did not see mentioned in 2004 was that there has been fighting along Sudan's western border dating from the 1970's. Several newspapers demanded an Iraq style of intervention by Western countries. This would have been totally disastrous and counter productive. None of the reports I have seen on the Darfur crisis attempt to analyse what is behind the actions of the government or the long-term causes. No journalist seems to be interested in getting to the roots of this humanitarian and environmental crisis which has gone on for around 30 years. If this "scar on the conscience of the world", as the British *Independent* put it on their front page on 21 August 2004, is to be healed we need journalists and aid organizations with a longer term view of Africa's problems. The media has a major role to play which at present it is failing to perform. Until this happens it may be necessary to be more selective in where journalists are sent. When aid is clearly requested by governments, the aid organizations and the media that follow them will be in a stronger position to take a long-term view. The best reporting we have seen of Darfur was by Nima el-Baghir, the *Reuters* correspondent in Khartoum. In an article in BBC Focus on Africa in October 2004 she uses interviews with a former defence minister. He is an African from Darfur and lives in a Khartoum suburb. However she is careful to talk in café's in Nyala and to the Popular Defence Force and does not exclusively use refugees as most of the other correspondents.

NOTES

1. How I found Livingstone. H.M. Stanley, London 1872.
2. Bearing Witness by Simon Haw 1996, *The Natal Witness*. Pietermaritzburg, page 67.
3. My interest in photography continued with in the main with slide film and transparencies. In the middle of the Air France hijack incident at Entebbe Airport (June 20th 1976) I had an urgent request for slides. I managed to find 2 or 3 of the old Airport and sent them to London by train from Swansea. They were used with many news programmes until the hostages were rescued on July 4th.
4. Mr Semana, the Head of Radio for Farmers under Idi Amin's rule gave me a warm welcome at Makerere University in 1996 where he was Head of the Department of Agricultural Extension and Education – my subject had been up-graded to a full department.
5. We got to know William in Zambia in the late 1970's when he was an exile with a large family after escaping from Uganda. In 1996 I met him at Makerere where he held a emeritus post in Zoology.
6. FEBA – Far East Broadcasting Association.
7. See later Chapter VII "The Lighter Side of Africa" for an account of the problems we had in extricating our tapes from Lusaka.

CHAPTER VI

Survivals from Colonial Rule

NO EMPIRE HAS existed which has had totally negative long-term effects on the peoples living under the rule of the colonialists. However in the heat of the struggle and ultimate liberation few people are likely to openly recognize the positive side. Over our 50 years in Africa and repeat visits to several countries like Kenya, South Africa, Zimbabwe and Zambia we have been able to experience many changes in life styles and attitudes. Memories of colonial days have faded in most countries but there are still physical reminders of "the old days". Statues, street signs and even buildings of obviously colonial designs stand out. When we spent some weeks in Moshi, Tanzania in 2000, while Theresa taught at the Kilimanjaro Christian Medical Centre (KCMC), I spotted the old Standard Bank building in town. Having been nationalized in 1967 the bank had been taken over by one of the State banks. It was impossible to disguise the stately Greek style columns along its front. It was presumably built in the 1930's when the Standard Bank of South Africa had branches throughout what was then British East Africa. On a recent bus trip from Nairobi to Moshi I spotted the brick shed where we signed our names in 1958 and 1961 when travelling on the same road. There was no immigration or customs in those days and the currency was the same – The East African shilling. Nowadays one can spend half a day negotiating the Kenyan and Tanzanian border posts – as I did in 1995. For several years this border was closed to traffic when relations between Kenya and Tanzania were bad.

There can be very few East Africans who remember the 1950's. However the signing on March 2nd 2004 of a Customs Union Protocol by the presidents of Kenya, Uganda and Tanzania was a hopeful sign that the 3 independent countries will one day come together again as they were in the East African Community days of the 1960's. Such close associations should be a help in avoiding dictatorial tendencies. In some ways I regret my support in 1958-60 for the campaign to break up the Central African Federation. Some of Robert Mugabe's more extreme actions that ruined the Zimbabwe economy would have been more difficult for him if the Federation had remained. It would have meant that he would have faced much more regional pressure to moderate his actions – something that has regrettably not happened at the time I'm writing. Details are given later in this chapter of how Tanzania has been re-privatising its banks.

It would be too much to expect African countries or their citizens to be enthusiastic about their colonial past. Yet many aspects of life, such as the language of the former rulers, survive in most of Africa where either English, French or Portuguese are still the Lingua Franca. The main exception, from the countries I have visited, would be the Sudan. I was sent there by Quaker Peace and Service in London during the major Sahara and Nile floods of 1988. In Khartoum senior officials still spoke excellent English. However at El Geneina, in West Darfur 500 miles away on the border of Chad, I had great difficulty in finding anyone in some offices who spoke English. I gradually learnt that, when confronted with a number of officials, to choose someone who had some white hair! Invariably I was warmly greeted and completed my business promptly.[1]

Sir William Rees Mogg[2] wrote recently in *The Times*: "Historic imperial nations, such as Turkey or Britain, know that empires always work between a balance of evils; they also know that no occupied country ever feels gratitude; nor should it". No one can expect gratitude – but I think Sir William overstates his case. As more and more African countries go through periods of economic collapse one nowadays does come across regrets that the stability of the colonial past has gone. In the Sudan there are very few people who remember the old days – pre 1956.

The most interesting country for a study of attitudes to colonial rule is the Republic of Cameroun. I have been there in 1955, 1958 and 1989. On the 1955 visit, after hitch-hiking on a WAIFOR[3] lorry to the Bamenda Agricultural Show, I managed to contact the family of a close student friend in London during 1953-54. His name is Victor Anomah Ngu and I have recently (2003) been in touch following his address to the 43rd Conference of the West African College of Surgeons held at the Nicon Hilton Hotel in Abuja, Nigeria. The link was re-established by a Nigerian surgeon, Shima Gyoh, who is convenor of a small group of Nigerian Quakers.

This is part of my diary for November 23-24th 1955:-

We arrived in Bamenda about 9.00 pm, after 3 days in the heat hitch-hiking from Abakaliki in Nigeria. "My bedroom was in the main building which had originally been the old German prison and had massive walls which kept it extremely cool even at midday. That night I slept like a log with 3 blankets and no mosquito net – the journey was worth it for that alone".

Next day "in the afternoon I wandered down to the lower town to try and look up the father of an old Hans Crescent[4] friend, Victor Ngu. … I enquired after his father at the UAC (United Africa Co.) store in the town and was guided down some narrow alleyways to a typical Bamenda house, a mud affair with a thatched roof. On this occasion his father had 'done gone for bush' or in other words had gone to the village in the hills that was presumably the original family home. However next day at the Show he came up to me and introduced himself in Pidgin English …. We had quite a long conversation and then on another day I called again at his house. It appears he had gone to one of the schools that the Germans set up when they came to Bamenda and had eventually become a clerk in the German court. When the Germans evacuated from Kamerun to the island of Fernando Po during the 1914-18 war he went with them but I gather soon returned to Bamenda. However he still appears to long for 'the good old days' and said he was one of the few Camerounians who preferred German to English rule. He said that the Germans were more efficient and got things done whereas the British dilly-dallied. He did admit, however, that in the process they committed a lot of brutal acts and he told how about a dozen Africans had died while constructing the road up to the station".

The sequel to this meeting with Mr. Ngu Senior is that in 1989, while working for IFAD in Yaounde I spent an evening with Victor and his Ghanaian wife. Victor was an academic genius, won several prizes studying surgery in Britain and eventually became Vice-Chancellor of the University of Yaounde. When we met he had just retired as Minister of Health. I told him about my discussions with his father and he said many of their problems were now blamed on the French! So for Victor's father the 'good old days' were German while for his son they were British! Maybe the next generation will say it was better under the French!

One interesting inheritance from German colonial rule (1884-1916) is Pidgin English. Although officially disapproved of it was still going strong in 1989 as a spoken language. I failed however to buy a Bible in Pidgin as I had hoped to do. John Gunther, in his book "Inside Africa", published in the 1950's, has a pidgin section from Genesis and claims in a footnote that German colonial officers were taught Pidgin in Berlin before being sent to West Africa. It was of course the Lingua Franca of much of the West Coast in the nineteenth century. A remarkable observation was that when I was entertained by a highly educated and completely bilingual family (English and French) in Bamenda the mother and daughters talked in Pidgin when they were in the kitchen! They explained that it felt more homely than the other languages they could have used. Another family I visited in Bamenda ran their own "in house" Chinese restaurant for parties of up to 10. The father had recently retired at age 50 after a spell as Ambassador to China – where his wife had learnt Chinese cookery. I regret not finding out what language they spoke in the kitchen! An unexpected and unpaid for bonus was to be entertained with tales of life in Beijing!

A topical colonial issue concerns the Australian tree Eucalyptus. Various species were introduced throughout the colonies by the British, French and Portuguese. The Benguela Railway in Angola was in 1958 still fuelled by wood. When I crossed Africa from Lobito to Mombasa by rail the engines ran on wood from huge gum plantations and the scent filled the carriages. The tree has recently been demonized by South Africa and various agencies for its fast growth and excessive use of water. My friend Victor told me how, when a school boy in the 1930's, he spent many hours a week collecting grass for his mother's stove. With the introduction of Eucalyptus they switched to cooking with wood. Translated to the whole of Africa a claim could be made for saying that Eucalypts saved millions of African indigenous trees from being cut for firewood. Incidentally, in South Africa, where some introductions were partly aimed at preventing mosquitoes from breeding, there are signs that mosquitoes and malaria are spreading to new areas where eucalypts have been removed.

Since buying the Welsh hill farm, Maesyreglwys (Meadow of the Church), in 1968 we have been based, during any longish periods out of Africa, in Wales. We have therefore been repeatedly exposed to the complications of multi-lingual societies. The Cameroun Republic is struggling to maintain several Bantu and Hamitic languages as well as both French and English. The Anglophone areas of the highlands bordering Nigeria are still a bastion of English. German has died out in Tanzania and, particularly in rural areas, English is likely to die out in the Sudan. A novel way of promoting bilingualism in Cameroun was to broadcast football commentaries on the radio alternately in 5 minutes of English and 5 minutes of French! Radio Wales could experiment with this approach for rugby matches! For Africa it seems that in most countries the languages of the former rulers will remain at least as dominant as they were before independence. One exception might be Tanzania, where great strides have been made in extending the use of Ki-Swahili through the education system. This had originally been spoken mainly along the coastal strip. I had direct experience of the unifying effect of Ki-Swahili when I taught at Makerere University, Uganda from 1966-72. We served the whole of East Africa so that a class would often consist of 11 Kenyans, 11 Ugandans and 11 Tanzanians of which 3 would usually be Asians. The 3 Tanzanian Asians would stand out for their interest in practicals, their ability to mix and work together and their proficiency in Ki-Swahili. A major contribution to their integration with their fellow Tanzanians had obviously been made by their having done compulsory national service. In those days Kenyans were more likely to speak Ki-Swahili than Ugandans.

Standards of English vary greatly across the former British colonies and protectorates. Much depends on the quality of the teachers and generally those countries with a high proportion of missionary teachers fared best. Catholic missions often had celibate teachers who were members of a holy order and cost much less to employ. They were usually the last teachers to be Africanised. When we filmed and presented a Lima Time television programme in the Barotse area of Zambia along the Zambezi I was struck by the excellent English of the Litunga's Prime Minister and other officials. It seemed to be partly the result of a series of missions which came to the area in the 1880's and 1890's. According to Peter Snelson[5] the largest contribution was made by the White Fathers. The first school in what became Zambia, was opened in the Barotse king's summer capital, Limulunga, in March 1883 by a Brethren missionary – but did not last long. An extraordinary fact is that the Paris Evangelical Missionary Society was forced by the Bourbons to work outside the French Empire. So many French-speaking missionaries helped to spread English across Africa. Snelson also reveals that Simon Kapwepwe, the first Vice-President of Zambia had his school fees paid by the local district commissioner when he came across the boy weeping while travelling on foot near Isoka. Kapwepwe's experience is a reminder of the tremendous thirst for education which has motivated Africans for well over a century. Long may it last! The most remarkable case was that of Kamuzu (meaning "little root") – Dr. Hastings Banda – who became the first Prime Minister of Malawi on February 1st 1963. At age 12 he set out on foot from a village in the north, of what was then Nyasaland, to walk to South Africa. After studying in the USA and Scotland he returned 35 years later to lead his country to independence. In view of his long career as a nationalist it is remarkable that he felt moved to start a school modelled on the British public schools. Called Kamuzu Academy, it taught Latin and Greek and selected staff with Oxford or Cambridge degrees. We happened to be working over the Zambian border in nearby St Francis Hospital when he was ousted in the 1994 election. The school survived but it is now for those whose parents can afford the fees – the Malawian elite.

One of the colonial hangovers of the British educational system in Africa is the continuing stress on every child wearing a uniform.[6] While at St. Francis Hospital, we got to know staff at the local Katete Secondary School. The 1994 school requirements included "maroon trousers or shirt, black polishable shoes, navy blue jerseys" and "a bucket for drawing water". When I helped to fill short-term gaps in the staff at Prince Edward School, Harare in 1991-3 the same uniform applied as when it had been an exclusively white school in the early 1970's. This included "a basher" or straw hat with purple band which had to be worn by boarders when going into town. Prince Edward School had been re-named in 1925 when the Prince of Wales (later King Edward) toured the British colonies. The government school kept up a tradition of performing a Gilbert and Sullivan opera every year long after Independence in 1980. Wiina Msamati, now a well known actor and son of a Tanzanian lecturer in medicine was a day boy at the school and a neighbour of ours in the Avondale university flats. When the Queen visited the school during the Commonwealth Conference in 1991 he performed as the Lord Chancellor, in a scene from Iolanthe, to perfection. Such a celebration would doubtless be seen by some as a decadent colonial hangover. However the aplomb with which it was performed must have swung over many critics. It was that Commonwealth meeting which adopted The Harare Declaration. This was later used to penalize Zimbabwe for a range of undemocratic acts against the opposition party the Movement for Multiparty Democracy (MMD).

Corporal punishment by caning might be considered a hangover from colonial times. However it was probably a milder form of punishment than what preceded it. Prince Edward, in my time in the 1990's, restricted it to the Headmaster and his deputy and it was certainly not allowed to be inflicted by prefects as was once the case in Britain. At about the same time as the Queen's 1991 visit the senior teacher of agriculture sent an entire class to be beaten for showing "a lack of interest"! My wife, while teaching at Moi University, Kenya in 1995 heard repeated slapping noises behind a hedge as she walked to the faculty one morning. She then saw a long line of school children being whacked by a teacher for being late. Several African countries have in recent years sought to reduce or even ban the use of corporal punishment. During a recent visit to Kenya we came across the problem again when there was a school heads meeting.[7] Mr. Patrick Monyenye, of the Head Teachers Association said the recent ban was "good in theory but practically it has failed to foster discipline among students". It is obviously a problem that has outlived colonial rule. It must be said however that even the raw "gap year" teachers that go out to Africa from Britain still find few problems with discipline compared with British schools.

Sport is a major inheritance of colonial times and there is no chance that games like football will not survive the departure of the colonialists. Prince Edward School in Harare[8] coasted for several years after independence on the reputation that Graeme Hick gave

Expensive cars for top officials have been a feature before and after independence. The Ki-Swahili term for the affluent –Wa-benzi – was coined from the frequent preference for Mercedes Benz after independence. In this pre-independence photo the Governor is getting into his official car after Sunday service in Nairobi Cathedral.
In the 1965 photo Vice-President Oginga Odinga rides out of Embu after showing his disapproval of such ostentation by walking 1-2 miles in 'Ahero' sandles (see page 50).

A 1960 photo of Adelaide Tambo and daughter at the London Missionary Society compound in Serowe, Bechuanaland after being flown from Swaziland where she had escaped after avoiding being arrested in the post-Sharpeville Emergency. A Ghana Airways DC3 collected her and over 20 other refugees from Francistown Airport.

Unrest in South Africa was sometimes sparked by 'removals' like that in Sophiatown which I witnessed in 1958 while staying at Trevor Huddleston's community in Johannesburg (see page 120).

Refugees have been a feature of African countries since pre-colonial times. Here our daughter Marguerite Mabathuse, who was born while we were working in Serowe, Bechuanaland, was visiting a Zionist group expelled from Rhodesia (see page 27). Fabrizio, a forester working for Quakers in West Darfur in 1988, is inspecting trees planted in a refugee camp for people fleeing Chad.

Rainfed cash crops, such as coffee, have made a great contribution to the economies of many African countries. This 1960's Muganda coffee farmer near Kampala in Uganda is clutching his visitors book and wears the traditional men's Kanga.

Farmers should benefit from moves to re-establish free trade in East Africa and hopefully congestion at border posts like this one at Namanga, between Nairobi and Arusha in Tanzania, will decrease.

This photo is of the Omukama of Toro, and his daughter Princess Elizabeth Bagaya, at a ceremony witnessed by my wife, Theresa, in 1956 at Fort Portal. The Princess, then a schoolgirl, was later appointed Foreign Minister by President Idi Amin.

A photo, taken in 1960, of the mother and child clinic Theresa started in our garden in Serowe. She had been told in the Imperial Reserve at Mafeking, then the capital of Bechuanaland, that they couldn't employ a woman doctor.

Nelson Nwosu, my first African friend from 1950, at the Umudike Agricultural Research Station near Umuahia, E. Nigeria, in 1955. His daughter Chioma visited us recently in Wales.

The Farewell Party on the 16th December 1957 when I was presented with a copy of the Nigeria Handbook by the staff of the Agricultural Station, Fashola, Oyo, "as a token of love and affection on the occasion of his departure from Nigeria on leave and retirement!" See page 46 for a discussion of Africanisation.

Our daughters, Marguerite and Kageha, trying out their 1965 Christmas presents in the garden of our house at Embu, Kenya. After being fostered Kageha had recently been adopted in the Kenya High Court and until 18 had a Kenya passport. Jeremy was born in 1966.
Visits to the UK were later spent on Maes-yr-eglwys, the Welsh hill farm we bought in 1968. Here Kageha and Jeremy are enjoying the farm pond with our dog.

This 1960 photo shows Molly and Guy Clutton-Brock inspecting an irrigated garden at Moeng College in Botswana. Guy had recently been released from prison in Rhodesia. Vernon and Tineke Gibberd worked with Guy at the nearby Radisele cooperative farming project. The Gibberds are now based in Queenstown, South Africa. The 'Hafir' system is based on what Vernon saw when he worked in the Sudan (see page 168). It involves a short channel from a road or path leading to an underground tank, covered to reduce evaporation. The water is pumped up to a small tank and then drip-fed to the plots. To increase soil fertility they have a compost toilet. Both systems badly need to be promoted throughout Africa.

*A 1960's photo of a school in Serowe which not only shows how poor
Botswana was before independence but also how cold the winter can be!
Botswana's current success is largely due to the fact that Cecil Rhodes et al
didn't know they had diamonds!*

*Jeptulu Primary School, next to Kaimosi Mission in Kenya, where I used to
teach an Extra-Mural class in Agriculture for Makerere University in 1963.
Roger Carter, a British Quaker, was addressing a gathering of the local
Salvation Army.*

Alfred Knottenbelt (holding large poster), a leading critic of the Smith Government, supported this Unity Square peaceful demonstration for peace in the Gulf shortly before his death. Theresa is on the right with other FOR members (see page 36).

Theresa and Martin Mansell from the Quaker Meeting in Harare investigate the removals to Porta Farm from Epworth. This was part of a 'clean up' for the 1991 Commonwealth Meeting. In a day of collecting signatures we managed to stop further evictions.

Members of the Trelawney Zimbabwe Commercial Farmers Union chat after a talk on land reform in Kenya and Zambia in 1992. See page 13 of Chapter II for details of talks and reactions.

Rainfed sugar, as here in KwaZulu/Natal, South Africa, can be converted from plantation production to small-holdings. In this project these two women were allocated plots in the late 1990's and were employing local men to do their cutting. The cane still has to be transported to the mill.

The Quaker Meeting House in Harare, Zimbabwe which we visited from Lusaka soon after the ceasefire at the end of 1979 and joined as members in 1990.

At the end of three months in Kisumu during 2004 when Theresa was teaching, we had a weekend in the Masai Mara Game Park and on the way noticed the Poroko Friends' Church. In the 60's she flew there every month with MAF to run a clinic. On our return we got a great welcome in their small church.

it for cricket. If independence hadn't come when he was in his early teens he would probably have played for Rhodesia or South Africa. In the end he decided to wait for several years to qualify for England. By the time he was selected he was past his prime, although as I write in 2004, he is still very highly rated in county cricket and a top scorer. Cricket will do well to survive the onslaught it has had in Zimbabwe during and following the World Cup Competition of 2003. The British media and some MP's played into the hands of the Zimbabwe government and allowed cricket to be used for political purposes. The ZANU/PF Government were able to say to the electorate that the western media were against them. Hopefully cricket will survive as potentially Zimbabwe should be one of the best cricketing nations in Africa. A major advantage is that many schools have cricket fields which are expensive for other countries which did not have a settler community.

I saw the potential of cricket as a sport soon after arriving in Nigeria in 1954. Few schools played the game partly because of the perennial problem of not having suitable flat land to play on. An exception was a remote new secondary school in an area north of Benin where the staff were keen on the game. I called there, on my way to inspect a primary teacher next day, in the middle of a cricket match. The star player was to be their first expatriate teacher. He had the misfortune to come from Yorkshire, then a leading cricketing country. Almost the entire senior staff had gone to collect him from the boat in Lagos and on his arrival a special staff versus student match was arranged. To his great embarrassment and the disappointment of the school his cricket skills were negligible! Being born in Yorkshire did not provide him with sufficient prowess to excel!

The potential of cricket showed up better in East Africa where there was usually a sprinkling of excellent local Asian players. That is until Idi Amin – who expelled virtually the entire Ugandan Asian population between August and December 1972. When I was sent by the UN to Kampala in 1975 the East African Quadrangular tournament was being held. The countries involved were Uganda, Kenya, Tanzania and Zambia. Uganda's team was all African, while Kenya and Zambia were mixed. The Tanzanian team of 16 were all Asian. 20 years later Uganda cricket has recovered from Amin's expulsions. A picture in a 1996 Uganda paper[9] had 4 Asians playing in the Bank of Baroda Cricket League Tie for the KICC (Kampala Indian Cricket Club). With still only a handful of schools playing cricket the game seems to be surviving in East Africa.

Idi Amin's love and hate affair with the British was founded on sports like boxing and rugby. I never heard of him playing cricket but he regularly played rugby before becoming President in the January 1971 coup.[10] Few people who were not in Uganda seem to remember that he was initially highly popular with the major tribe, the Baganda – and the British. The Baganda because they hated President Obote for his removal of their king, the Kabaka, from power in May 1966. The British, because of President Obote's threats before and during the 1971 Commonwealth Conference around the issue of Apartheid in South Africa. At the High Commission's 1970 Christmas Party the talk amongst the British community was about how long we all had before we lost our jobs. In practice there was a relatively peaceful 18 month period. In March 1972 I was commissioned to organize a conference on the promotion of air freight exports of vegetables and flowers. We left Uganda soon afterwards when the country was quiet. I was at the end of my 6 year contract which provided for rail and boat travel to UK. There were no forewarnings of the disasters that lay ahead although an article I wrote in the Uganda Argus on the Asian contribution to farming coincided with one of Amin's early anti-Asian speeches.

The date of the coup was shortly before Uganda was due to celebrate the fiftieth anniversary of what was originally called Makerere College. By October 7 1972 when the Graduation Ceremony was performed Idi Amin was Chancellor. Dr. William Lamont, the senior surviving British principal, was invited to give a public lecture. Abu Mayanja, who had been expelled by the British principal, when a student, for his involvement in disturbances, gave a lecture on "Makerere's Contribution to East Africa and Beyond". At the time of his expulsion Governor Sir Andrew Cohen, had recognised his ability during the pre-independence period and helped to get him a scholarship to Cambridge.

Another ceremony involved a survival of the Empire which had made great contributions to the expansion of Uganda's economy. In 1921 the Empire Cotton Growing Corporation was founded to promote cotton growing and research which after the war involved

Uganda. Idi Amin officiated at the hand-over of the Namulonge Cotton Research Station outside Kampala. Sir Joseph Hutchinson, the first director and a leading British scientist, came out from Britain to hand over the station on January 5th 1972 and we were invited to the ceremony. Idi welcomed the Ugandan employees into government service – after sweeping past the refreshments provided because it was a Muslim festival and he was fasting! His mainly non-Muslim entourage had to join the fast until later in the day! In his speech he stressed the beauty of the place. He said: "I would like to warn Ugandans of this station's cleanliness, discipline and efficiency which the British have established. This must be maintained and improved. I don't want to see this beautiful place grow bushy and untidy". He mentioned that some Ugandans "allowed standards to drop". On a return visit to the station in 1975 on my UN passport I found the place "bushy and untidy". More seriously cotton was no longer a major crop partly because the Asians who ran the textile industry had been expelled. When I met the Director he desperately wanted to find a job outside Uganda.

We have found the demonisation of individual African dictators by the British media inaccurate, distorted and distasteful. In the case of Idi Amin he received a very inadequate education.[11] This could have helped him to provide better leadership. His army training in Africa and Britain was not appropriate. The atrocities he undoubtedly committed were the result of the increasingly narrow tribal base of his government. A high proportion of those killed were due to over-zealous personnel in the Army and Security Forces. On taking over he promised free elections and appointed a string of the best qualified Ugandans to the key ministries. For a time it looked as if he might pull off his take over. He even told his soldiers not to pull down the 2 metre bronze medallion of Obote hanging at the entrance to Parliament. He said that is part of Uganda's history! He restored the Grand Hotel to the old name – Imperial[12] – on the same grounds! All started to fall apart when Obote, with Nyerere's support, built up an army to invade and re-establish the former regime. Several Ugandans have told me that if that had not happened Amin could have survived longer and the country would have been more peaceful.

In November 1971 Idi made a great impression when visiting the University Farm Open Day outside Kampala. Invitations had been declined by Obote in previous years presumably because of Baganda opposition. When his Minister of Agriculture called informally in the 1960's a gun fell out of his pocket when he bent down to tie his shoe lace. Idi was in an ebullient mood and even rode a bicycle cart with a Minister in the back that had been developed at the farm. At the 3 two hectare research small-holdings I ran with peasant farmers as tenants he sparkled with interest and kept spotting things he wanted to see at close quarters. I was even able to argue with him over his idea to start one in the semi-desert district of Karamoja! His coup proved to be a total disaster within 18 months and his dream that he should expel the Asians completely wrecked the economy. His experiences in the KAR[13] and his commanding officers' training course in Wiltshire U.K. do not seem to have provided an adequate education for presidential duties. The colonial and British military skills he acquired were inadequate for running a modern African state. Perhaps, if he had taken a long walk at age 12 to get a university education, like Kamuzu Banda of Malawi, Uganda might have escaped some of the horrors of his period in power. Britain would have been saved some embarrassing accusations because of its lack of support for what (in spite of its acute defects) was the duly elected government of Dr. Obote. In retrospect Idi Amin's period in power was not an edifying example of colonial survivals.

We have close attachments to the next door state to Uganda – Kenya. We both made visits in the 1950's and, after we married, worked there for 4 years in the 1960's and 2 years in the 1990's. Our daughter Kageha was born there near Vihiga in 1961 and was later fostered and finally adopted by us. We made many visits from Uganda from 1966-72 and from Zambia (1977-86) when our daughter studied there at Kianda College, Nairobi. We were even there, by chance just after the abortive coup against President Arap Moi in 1982. We were attending a Quaker gathering from around the world at our former mission – Kaimosi. The idea was that our children would join us there prior to a holiday near Malindi. Kageha was booked on a London – Nairobi – Seychelles flight which overflew Nairobi because of the coup. With a restricted ticket she took 2 weeks to get a refund so as to join us.

On a recent visit in March 2004 I was able to reacquaint myself with the Cathedral Church of the Province of Kenya in Nairobi. I had last attended a service there in 1958 and have a photo of

Governor Rennison, entering his official car at the cathedral entrance. This time we went to hear my student friend Donald Thomas sing with a German choir in celebration of the 35th Anniversary of the German school. He became a Kenyan citizen after independence and has contributed greatly to his country's development as a civil servant, dairy and strawberry farmer, professor of agricultural engineering and in the Quaker church in Nairobi.

In the Cathedral, during an interval, I noticed some of the plaques which commemorate colonial battles. In both World Wars the battles between the British, German or axis forces involved Kenyans. From the 1914-18 war there is a plaque to the 250 Kenya African Rifles (KAR) soldiers who died in the East African campaign chasing the Germans out of German East Africa – now known as Tanzania. The 1939-45 war plaque commemorates those who died in Northern Kenya, Somalia and Ethiopia. In view of the partly German audience it was interesting to find a plaque to Capt. Baron von Offert, M.C. KAR who died on 7/8/1923 – presumably after serving on the British side.

Our 2 years (1995-6) at Moi University, Eldoret, where Theresa was a professor, enabled us to meet several old colonial, retired settlers. One was Nancy Riley, dairy farmer, who with her husband passed their farm to their manager on condition that they and their son could retain the house for their lifetimes. Another was a farm manager for Mr. Nicholas Biwott, a leading politician. On Saturdays his job was to sign in his bosses' visitors in the Club. He had come out as a settler from Derbyshire and farmed until independence when he was bought out by the government.

In his epic work "Empire"[14] Niall Ferguson lists 9 important features of what the British introduced in a country they governed. They were:-

"The English language
English forms of land tenure
Scottish and English banking
The Common Law
Protestantism
Team Sports
The limited or 'night watchman' state
Representative assemblies
The idea of liberty".

We have already covered some of these features and do not need to cover them again. Land Tenure will be covered in another chapter which includes agriculture. Banking is a specialized subject but has been mentioned in connection with the nationalisation in Tanzania during 1967. Protestantism is in effect covered in the chapter on religion. We have very positive memories of the role of Catholic missions as regards education, health services and agriculture. A major plus for the Catholics is their long-term commitment to projects and a much longer hand-over period following the granting of independence. Team sports are well covered in this chapter. The main problem of the limited or 'night watchman' state is a too rapid withdrawal and this will be well covered in several chapters. Representative assemblies and the idea of liberty will be dealt with in the chapter on disasters – which involves the numerous failures of democracies in Africa.

It can be mentioned here that as of now some of Tanzania's "colonial" banks have come back through the Parastatal Sector Reform Commission (PSRC). By 2003 "326 state-owned farms" had been privatised with only 14 being 100% foreign owned. Amongst the partly foreign owned banks are Barclays, "the 19th commercial bank" to be licensed to resume operations. More and more financial institutions involve South Africa. The ABSA Group finally paid 18.75 US million dollars to the Tanzanian Treasury on 30 March 2000 for a stake in the National Bank of Commerce.[15]

My main brush with common law in Nigeria was when I hit the back of a lorry belonging to my own department in the heart of Ibadan's slums. Although this was in 1957 and well before full independence the magistrates were nearly all Nigerian. I wrote home on 4 Dec. 1957:-

> "I was eventually charged for the car accident I had. They had warned me at the time that, if an accident is reported then 'someone's got to be summonsed' and if you hit another vehicle you are in the wrong whatever the circumstances. I went for advice to Bank Oki, an old tennis acquaintance who is also a Queens Counsel. He advised me to plead guilty and emphasize the mitigating circumstances. Pleading not guilty here involves endless adjournments. ...... If you are hit by a taxi ...... you stand very little chance of getting off – many of the taxis are owned by the police! ..... One poor chap in Ibadan who hit the

back of a taxi which stopped without warning was fined £10 and had his license endorsed. An African brought up the same day for knocking someone down in the road and not reporting it was fined a pound".

These comments on the law represent a typical "colonial" view at the time. However I don't remember any great resentment at the way I was treated. What hurt more was the fact that my vehicle was the one that was damaged. The lorry had hardly a scratch! However that is the law everywhere. I was eventually fined a fairly nominal amount by a Nigerian woman magistrate when I appeared for the second time, the first having been adjourned.

A further brush with the law took place in Wales in 1972-73 when we found that former Justice Jeffreys Jones, a Puisne Judge of the Uganda High Court, had just retired down our valley. He had spent over 20 years in Uganda after becoming Senior Resident Magistrate in 1950. There was little interest in Uganda in the Swansea Valley so he seemed glad of our visits to The Larches, the house where he lived with his sister. Although a quiet bachelor he came to the fore in Uganda when he headed a "Commission of Inquiry into missing Americans, Messrs. Stroh and Siedle". We had met Siedle who attended our Quaker meeting and was a lecturer in Makerere University. They were last seen in Mbarara Rest House and had gone to the barracks of the Simba Battalion on the 8th July 1971 to investigate some shooting that had been heard. Jones stated in the Commission report[16] that "It was becoming apparent that the Army considered themselves to be above the law". He adjourned the Inquiry "indefinitely". "On the night of the 6th April 1972 I was telephoned by His Excellency, who expressed his displeasure that I had not informed him of the intended adjournment". The main breakthrough came with an affidavit sworn by Lieut. Silver Tibihika which reported the deaths and the way the bodies were disposed of and how their car was dumped in the Ruwenzori Mountains. According to Denis Hills in his book The White Pumpkin[17] Major Juma Ali "was notoriously involved in killing 2 Americans in Mbarara barracks". Jones was warned by the British High Commissioner of Amin's likely displeasure when the report was published and advised it should not be handed to him in Uganda.

91

David Jeffreys Jones' story of how he concluded his inquiry and managed to leave Uganda unscathed was remarkable. The case had aroused great interest in the American and Canadian press and Amin was under great pressure. Jeffreys told us how he decided to proceed on retirement leave before the report went to Amin. At the Tororo border post the man on the barrier seemed to recognize Jones' car and ran to the offices. For a dreadful moment Jones thought they had been told to send them back to Kampala to face the President. There was then a huge anti-climax when the guard reappeared with his cap on and gave them a salute. He had forgotten to wear his cap!

Denis Hills has some interesting observations on Idi Amin's respect for the Queen. Of course he later was close to losing his life by firing squad. Idi Amin was enraged by his views in the book "The White Pumpkin". He was saved by diplomatic pressure and the visit of Mr. Callaghan to Uganda. Amongst the Amin quotes he has in his book are:-

"The Queen is my friend"

"The missionaries were good people".

He drew attention to the fact that Amin was "amicably received by the British government in London and by the Queen" soon after the 1971 coup.

In retrospect the British involvement in Uganda during the regime of Idi Amin was embarrassing. Both Israel and Britain made some early decisions to support him that they must have soon regretted. The book[18] by Judith Listowel gives some extraordinary detail of what happened when Britain laid out the red carpet for him in July 1971:

"When the Queen asked him what he hoped most to get out of his visit, the General apparently replied, 'A pair of size fourteen boots and a Scottish pipe major to teach my chaps to play the bagpipes'. The Queen offered to supply the piper, whom Amin could choose from Balmoral. (This he did, and the Scotsman travelled with him back to Uganda – again via Tel Aviv)".

While there is much which appears to be humourous to outsiders about Amin's rule for Ugandans his rule was overall a huge disaster. However, the British and Ugandan governments pre-Amin share a considerable responsibility for Amin's rise to a point where he was able to bring off a coup and remain in power for so many years. We were in Kenya in 1964 when there was a succession of mutinies in Tanzania, Kenya and Uganda. While in Kenya and Tanzania the governments were able to re-assert their authority, in Uganda British officers were soon replaced and Amin was placed on a course to eventually take over the government from Obote.

A remarkable survival of Empire through many African countries is the Agricultural Show. Probably one of the first is what is still known as the Pietermaritzburg Royal Show which in 2003 celebrated 152 years with an attendance of 222,000 visitors.[19] Shows were started to promote excellence in livestock and other farm products. Kenya had a series of shows throughout the country organized originally mainly by settlers through the Agricultural Society of Kenya (ASK). The then Prince of Wales toured Southern Africa in 1925 and a highlight was the Kafue Show in Northern Rhodesia.[20] It was the sixth staged by the show society and was an entirely settler and colonial government affair. Since most settlers travelled then by ox wagon many Africans, who had been involved in driving ox wagons and leading animals, would also have seen the show. A history of the Zambian shows has a line of Hereford cattle belonging to Mopani Clarke each led by a herdsman to the show.[21] Following Independence on January 22 1964 there was a gradual Africanisation of show proceedings. The 1965 show was opened by Emperor Haile Selassie of Ethiopia and in 1967 Sir Seretse Khama, the President of Botswana was invited. In September 1959 Theresa and I went to work with Seretse in the capital of his tribe, the Bamangwato. My post was Tribal Agricultural Officer and one of my jobs was to revive their Agricultural Show which had been discontinued for several years. This was following Seretse's marriage to Ruth Williams which led to his being exiled by the British government on February 5th 1950.

When we spent several weeks helping at the Tropical Institute of Community Health in Kisumu, Kenya recently (March 2004) agricultural shows were in the news. They seem to survive changes of government well. In the 1990's, when Theresa worked at Moi University, Eldoret we attended the ASK show which we had also attended in 1962 – before Independence. Back then the British Army flew in soldiers from Aden for a parade and the survivors of the Afrikaans speaking farmers came in an ox-drawn wagon.

The 1962 parade with the Boer farmers wives wearing bonnets was a final fling – but some of the community are still there. Farnie Kruger recently organized a farmers' demonstration over prices and others worked for Nicholas Biwott when we lived there. In 2004 a farmers' protest demonstration during President Kibaki's opening of the show was denied a licence. Another news item was concerned with land disputes involving properties owned by the Agricultural Society of Kenya. The last European secretary of the Society reported in 1969[22] that they were then staging 10 shows per annum and had "3,800 members of all races".

During our recent 2½ months in Kisumu we stayed for several weeks at an old colonial survivor – The Nyanza Club. We had joined the Club in 1962 when we went to work at the nearby Kaimosi Quaker mission as a teacher trainer and doctor. Our main interest was in the swimming pool and it was there that we encountered what might be called the most unacceptable face of colonialism. The Club had a membership clause which specifically mentioned race and we had the extraordinary experience of being told our fostered baby, Kageha, was not allowed to lie on the lawn on a towel. The rule was abandoned at Independence but must have caused great offence to Asians and Africans for years. Nowadays the majority of members are Asian mainly because they are better placed to pay the substantial membership fees.

The history of the Club has been recorded in some detail up to 1990.[23] Changes in the rules were hard fought over for many years. On 11th May 1959 it was agreed in principle there would be open nights two times a year "to which non-whites could be invited". On 20th March 1962 they turned down a request from the Dar-es-Salaam Club for reciprocity over Dar's decision to go multi-racial. Once this was conceded membership boomed from 110 full members in 1963 to 650 in 1979.[24] Clubs throughout British colonies and even more so in Rhodesia were the last bastions of exclusivity. We stayed recently in the prestigious Bulawayo Club as guests of Professor Terence Ranger. We were astonished to find a list of colonial-style dress regulations on the door. It had recently been enforced by the door keeper when an open meeting was held for potential emigrants to New Zealand. The walls were a veritable cornucopia of old colonial pictures. The pioneer column of 1890, Cecil Rhodes at the opening of the first bowling green in

Southern Africa (1896) plus Queen Victoria and Winston Churchill.

A remarkable colonial hangover is that of dress. The extent to which it occurs has varied considerably in different countries. On the other hand local styles of dress were developed and even encouraged in several countries. We are most familiar with the basuti – the woman's dress favoured amongst the Baganda. This was reportedly encouraged by early Church Missionary Society missionaries. Another was the very distinctive Herero Victorian style dress worn by the people of that tribe who were persecuted in German South West Africa during the battles for their homeland with the German invaders in the 1890's. When we lived in the Bechuanaland Protectorate (now Botswana) from 1959-61 we often saw their stately women walking down the main dirt road through Serowe. Many Herero lived in exile until Namibian Independence in 1990.

The BBC publication *Focus on Africa* recently carried 3 articles[25] on fashion in politics covering South Africa, Kenya and Nigeria. Fred Khumalo claims that Nelson Mandela "revolutionized fashion in parliament" by replacing drab western style suits with gay shirts worn without a jacket. According to Oyunga Pala: "Today's Kenyan statesman is a person dressed in a dark suit and white shirt". Apparently the Speaker, Francis ole Kaparo, evicted some members of parliament from the house when they appeared in new African styles of dress. In contrast, according to Sola Odunfa, in Nigeria "politicians must discard their foreign dresses the minute they assume office".

Kenya's adoption of Western dress may make a little sense in Nairobi, where the mornings and evenings can be quite chilly. But in Kisumu on the shore of Lake Victoria, where we lived for several weeks in February and March 2004, it is surely absurd. The open air market on the Kakamega Road still has several stalls selling up to 100 second hand dark suits. District Commissioners and other government staff still wear the colonial style pith helmets that stopped being compulsory wear in most of Africa long before I joined the Colonial Service in 1953. An exception was Dr. Albert Schweitzer in his mission hospital at Lambaréné on the west coast of Africa. He insisted on even visitors wearing one in the 1960's. John Gunther[26] described the welcome of the Doctor when he arrived at the mission by government launch as follows:-

"He asked us, horrified, why we were not wearing sun-helmets. We discovered later that sun helmets are practically a fetish at Lambaréné ..... At least a dozen times in the next few days people rushed after us every time we stepped out, offering us the headgear". Gunther later explained that "sun helmets are completely archaic in most parts of Africa, but not here. There is a good reason for this. The sun helmet is the badge of the old colonial". Presumably the first President of Kenya, Jomo Kenyatta, must have retained a grudging respect for the British administration service that he fought against for so long!

As I write in July 2004 there is another extraordinary colonial hangover from Botswana. According to *The Times* correspondent[27] in Johannesburg a High Court case was starting in Gaborone, Botswana, involving 200 Bushmen or Basarwa. They are appealing a decision to remove them from the Central Kalahari Game Reserve. The South African lawyer, representing them, is basing their case on the fact that when the reserve was established in 1961 the British Government ruled the country. We lived there at the time and regularly saw Basarwa shopping in Serowe. In fact my superior, Seretse Khama, then Secretary of the Bamangwato Tribal Administration, employed many Basarwa to look after his huge herds of cattle at Nata.

While we were in Kenya this year another historic colonial legal case was receiving a great deal of publicity. This was the 1929 treaty between Britain and Egypt which prohibited commercial use of Lake Victoria's waters by East African countries. With populations expanding, regular droughts and food shortages it is hoped that some of this resource can be used. I had previously gone into the issue in 1964 when I wrote a feature article for the *East African Standard* on the question of flooding around the lake. The local people were blaming it on the Owen Falls Dam, opened in April 1954 by the then Queen Elizabeth, the mother of the present Queen. I found out that 2 Egyptian engineers permanently monitored the outflow. Furthermore the authorities claimed that the dam was designed to let through exactly as much water, when fully opened as would have gone through before the dam was built. I had no means of verifying this information! In 2004 control of the dam is still a hot subject and many international meetings will be needed to sort it out. One interesting piece of information is that

80% of the water in the lake goes up into the air with evaporation. Whatever the true situation a very small percentage of the water in Lake Nasser must derive from Lake Victoria.

Making return visits to a number of countries after they have obtained independence has enabled me to identify survivals from the colonial period. It is clear that they are many and varied. They are much more in evidence in countries that have had settled government since the 1960's when they received independence. Coups, as in Uganda, major changes of direction as in the case of Ujamaa in Tanzania and even short periods of violence, as in Lesotho, are all destabilizing. It is surprising how much of the physical infrastructure has survived. While some statues, commemorative plaques and road name plates have been changed many have survived. I recently asked a Nigerian friend in Benue State "who was Captain Downes?" That is the name of his road. He replied that it was the name of an early colonial administrative officer! If his road name plate has survived a 100 years perhaps it may survive another 100!

A colonial survival which will not go away for centuries is that of international boundaries. Our son spotted a cut-price book[28] in an Oxford shop in the 1990's which I frequently refer to whenever there is a border crisis. It is a mine of information covering the whole of Africa. The border that is in the news as I write (August 2004) is that between Sudan and Chad. I was sent there to a Quaker project in refugee camps at El Geneina in 1988 when the main problem was flooding. The refugees were then from Chad. In 2004 the problem is even more complicated with camps on both sides of the border. Accusations of genocide have tended to cloud the real issue and diverted attention from long-term solutions. Many African borders are unmarked or controlled in any way and in El Geneina there was plenty of evidence of the camel trains that were said to be a major channel for smuggling gum Arabic from Sudan to Chad. Border problems are accentuated by the massive growth of populations since independence. According to Stanton[29] the population of Sudan had grown from 10 million in 1956 to 30 million in 2000 while Chad grew from 3 million to 7 million.

Population and border issues will be dealt with in a later chapter on disasters. It will also discuss the question of how far the colonial powers can be blamed for all the problems arising from the borders inherited by the states that became independent. The question of blame and reparations for such evils as slavery, which were sometimes part of colonial rule, will also be discussed. As an agriculturalist, for me a major positive contribution has been the promotion of export crops such as cotton, cocoa, coffee and tea. Export crops have been denigrated by some aid bodies such as War on Want, because it is claimed these crops divert farmers from food production. I am convinced they have had an overall beneficial effect and in fact the countries like Kenya, which have had a good record in export crops, also manage to feed themselves better than many other countries which have been confined to growing food crops only.

NOTES

1. An interesting bit of advice which revealed some memories of the old regime came from a Greek trader I met when walking in the desert near the old wartime airport. He warned me of the dangers of being kidnapped by some of the unruly tribes in the mountains. If I was he recommended that I tell my captors that I belong to Mr. Moore's tribe. Much later I discovered that Guy Moore was the District Commissioner of Kutum in the 1930's. He rode a camel, wore local dress, spoke fluent Arabic and identified with the people in his care. He was obviously still fondly remembered long after his death.
2. *Times* 17/5/04.
3. WAIFOR = West African Institute for Oil Palm Research, Benin, Nigeria.
4. Hans Crescent was in the 1950's a British Council hostel for students from Africa, etc. It reserved a small percentage of rooms for British students preparing to work overseas. Situated behind the prestigious Harrods store it was near to Hyde Park where I once played football for a student British Empire team versus the Rest of the World!
5. Educational Development in Northern Rhodesia 1883-1945 by Peter Snelson. Kenneth Kaunda Foundatiion, Lusaka, 1974.
6. A plus for the uniform rule in schools is that it has helped village seamstresses to survive in many parts of Africa. Without it they would have long ago succumbed to what in Zambia is called Salaula – secondhand clothing from Europe and the USA.
7. Caning ban a headache for teachers, Alfred Oduor. E.A. Standard 18/3/04.
8. It is interesting that old boys were known as old Hararians in colonial times. Houses were still named Rhodes, Jameson etc. in the 1990's.

9. New Vision, Kampala 17/6/96.
10. According to "Amin" by Judith Listowel (IUP Books, Dublin, 1973) he was the only African member of the Jinja Rugby Club and on January 30 1971 he had 500 men on the barracks playing field to teach them rugby.
11. Idi Amin Dada was born in 1925 on the Sudan border and belonged to a mainly Sudanese tribe, the Kakwa. He received only primary education and was then recruited into the King's African Rifles (KAR) to serve against the Mau Mau in Kenya. His promotion was the result of accelerated Africanisation by both the British and President Obote's government.
12. Now known as The Grand Imperial Hotel.
13. Kings African Rifles.
14. Empire: how Britain made the modern world by Niall Ferguson. Allen Lane/Penguin, London, 2003 page xxii.
15. Tanzanian Affairs issued by the Britain Tanzanian Society No. 66.
16. Republic of Uganda, Part I and Part II Reports of Commission of Inquiry. Govt. Printer, Entebbe 1972.
17. The White Pumpkin by Denis Hills – George Allen & Unwin, London, 1973.
18. Amin by Judith Listowel, IUP Books, Dublin, 1973, page 95.
19. Farmers Weekly, 1st August 2004.
20. Show Time – A history of the Zambia Agricultural and Commercial Society, 1914-76 by Dick Hobson, 1979.
21. The Black and White in Southern Zambia, 1890-1930 by Kenneth Vickery & Greenwood Press Inc., Westport, Conn claims ox ploughing was adopted by Tonga peasant farmers in the 1930's after they had learnt the skills working for the local settlers (pages 159-171).
22. New Hope for Rural Africa. Ed. By E.R. Watts, E.A. Publishing house, Nairobi, 1969.
23. Nyanza Club. 75th Anniversary Monograph 1915-1990.
24. There is a plaque in the grounds which was unveiled by the then Minister for Tourism on the 28th of April 1990.
25. Focus on Africa. Vol. 15, No. 3, July 2004.
26. Inside Africa by John Gunther. Hamish Hamilton, London, 1955, page 708.
27. Michael Dynes, *The Times*, July 6 2004.
28. Malcolm Shaw. The Title to Territory in Africa, Clarendon Press, 1986, Oxford.
29. William Stanton. The Rapid Growth of Human Populations 1750-2000. Multi-Science Publishing Co. Ltd. Brentwood, Essex, UK, 2003.

CHAPTER VII

The Lighter Side of Africa

SOON AFTER WE moved to a flat in Avondale, a suburb of Harare in 1990 the Rhodesian-born author Doris Lessing published a book entitled "African Laughter".[1] I had been looking for something that would explain to me what makes the people of the continent so cheerful. I hoped for a few laughs for myself as well. I was disappointed. She explained that the African laughter of the title was the laughter of poor people. In reviewing the book David Morgan quotes[2] her speaking in New York: "Far from weeping in their huts, they are in there fighting, without proper water and proper food". She contrasted "Zimbabwe with Kenya, where the slums of Nairobi stretch as far as the eye can see and nobody gives a damn". In contrast Zimbabwe has now followed the economic collapse of neighbours like Mozambique and Zambia whose economies are now starting to improve. The amazing thing is that even in the most depressing run down slum there is still laughter. What disappointed me in the book was that there was no explanation of what makes such poor people laugh.

A recent letter from a Nigerian Quaker states:

"We survive here by our sense of humour. We are good at laughing at ourselves. People who cannot get enough food to eat, and who watch their children die ..... mourn today, but soon learn to laugh again".

The Nigerian papers have been carrying a story set in Hell involving an American, a Briton and a Nigerian. They all asked the Devil for permission to phone home and were charged at different rates. The American paid a 1000 dollars for 10 minutes, the Briton paid 1000 pounds for 15 minutes and the Nigerian paid twenty naire for 2 hours – then worth very little. The American and the

100

Brit cried foul. How can he pay so little for a much longer call? The Devil, with an impish smile and twitching his moustache replied: "You both made international calls but the Nigerian was making a local call!"

In seeking for Africa's lighter side I have tried to laugh with rather than at. Laughing at people can in certain contexts be upsetting and lead to misunderstandings. I first had the feeling of laughing with Nigerians when in 1956 I sat with a group of students in a Lagos flat – some of whom were on the committee of the Student Christian Movement of Nigeria with me. They were discussing their feelings on returning to the privations of Lagos after studying in Britain. They were good humoured but critical of the lack of facilities, poor transport, the humid heat and the rubbish in the streets.

It was about the time that I read Doris Lessing's book that I got launched into what the government newspaper *The Herald* called its Lighter Look column in the Saturday edition. Prior to 1980 *The Herald* had of course been the *Rhodesian Herald* and was a major supporter of the Ian Smith and Muzorewa governments. I had written occasional feature articles for it since my arrival 10 years after independence. I went to the deputy editor's office to chase up a lost article I had written on the crop tobacco, then the main source of foreign exchange for the country. World Health campaigns to reduce tobacco consumption were being vigorously denounced by the white farmers. Since the article was quite negative I joked as I was leaving the office: "*The Herald* presumably has a mole whose main job is to lose articles undermining the tobacco industry!" As I was getting to the lift the deputy Editor shouted for me to come back. He then said: "You seem to have a sense of humour, why don't you try writing some of the 'Lighter Look' columns!" Since it would give me an opportunity to get into print on some of the more serious issues I was interested in I took up the challenge. I have little idea of my eventual readership but noticed that the paper still carried the sort of advertising that it had before it was controlled by ZANU PF. This implied the paper still had a substantial white readership. My columns probably appealed to them more than the majority.

Humour doesn't come easily in a country like Zimbabwe in a mixed racial situation such as a newspaper read by both black and white. Lenny Henry,[3] the black British comic, who is of West Indian origin, implies he was careful not to use his humour on the mainly white teachers at his school in Dudley, near Birmingham. He admits to teasing a martinet teacher with a booming voice and once had a beating. Now that he is well known he can use his status as a comedian to help Africans overcome the negative image of their continent. He also admits to being popular, as one of 6 black boys in the Blue Coat Secondary Modern School, because he could impersonate white people. Doris Lessing in her book 'African Laughter' gives a few examples of taking off white people. She recalls giving an old African man a lift on the way to Mutare. They discussed the name changes of towns which had started in the 1980's. Her passenger laughed about forgetting the new name and using the old name – Umtali – or even Salisbury for the capital. "You'll be reported to the comrades"!, he had been warned! "Soon only old people like me will remember!" "And he shook with laughter, the marvelous African laughter born somewhere in the gut, seizing the whole body with good humoured philosophy" (page 80). When I helped Zambian television with a farming programme in the 1980's this "good humoured philosophy" saw us through several annoying incidents of lateness or equipment failure. When I met the Producer, Alfred Kalonga, we always exchanged an African double handshake preceded by a slap! – and grinned at each other.

One doesn't hear the expression "Darkest Africa" much nowadays. But in most Westerners minds Africa is not a humourous place. Indeed when Europeans hear that someone is being sent to Africa, other than to a beach resort or wildlife safari, the response is often one of commiseration. The media have saturated us with images of starving children, adults dying of AIDS and drought stricken crops. Yet whenever I have been to Africa by boat or plane my spirit has been lifted by the people and the smiles that invariably welcome a new arrival. Smiles are even stronger when one meets an old colleague or friend. We were amazed in 2004 to return to Kaimosi in Kenya, where we lived from 1962-65 and be remembered by an old colleague at the Teacher Training College. This was Crispus Sultani who had retired to his home village, Jeptulu in 1991 after a career which took him all over Kenya. Theresa was working as a doctor in the Hospital when his wife had a baby in 1963. He met her in 2004 while cycling on the road through the campus and amazingly remembered her christian name. We had a cheerful exchange of news of old colleagues and farmers.

The Kaimosi incident brought back memories of another unexpected meeting on the main road from Nairobi to Kampala in the late 1960's before it was tarmaced. There was a lot of loose gravel and suddenly our windscreen shattered into small pieces. A man who was struggling through the dust to cycle on the other side of the road dismounted gracefully and got off his bike. He greeted us with a broad smile and said "Good afternoon, Mr. Watts!" It then transpired that he was a local teacher and had been taught by me. We were about 50 miles from the college but continued at a slower pace to Kampala minus a windscreen. Fortunately it didn't rain and we were able to get a new one next day. The BBC correspondent Kate Adie is reported to have claimed when summing up her career covering trouble spots and disasters that she never became despairing or depressed. There were always enough examples of fortitude and willingness to share with others for her faith in the human race to be restored. Many of her assignments were in Africa's toughest trouble spots. In our experience good humour and even joking would be the major response even in times of tragedy.

The fact that Africans throughout the continent speak several languages gives opportunities for humour when they are mis-used or used in an unconventional manner. An early example was the letter "Love on the Line" published in the Pioneer's Scrapbook.[4] The British find great humour in the way foreigners use English, as Gerard Hoftnung's use of Austrian landladies letters in his famous speech to the Oxford Union showed. This poetic but humourous mis-use is not strictly African but took place on African soil:-

"Most honoured and respected Sir, I have the honour to humbly and urgently require your Honour's permission to relieve me of my onerous duties ... so as to enable me to visit the land of my nativity, to wit India, for sooth. This is in order that I may take unto wife a damsel of many charms who has long been cherished in the heartbeats of my soul ...... said beauteous damsel has long been goal of my manly breast and now am fearful of other miscreant deposing me .... If for reasons of state, the presence cannot suitably comply .... Then I pray your most excellent Superiority to grant me this benign favour for Jesus

Christ's sake, a gentleman your Honour very much resembles. I have the honour to be .... Your most humble and dutiful, but terribly lovesick mortal withal Signed Station Master". THE REQUEST WAS GRANTED!

This Asian station master could have applied to Gilbert and Sullivan to become a script writer. An African example of a similar use of flowery English came from the end of year (1993) message of Dr. Mtonga, the Eastern Province Permanent Secretary when we lived at St. Francis Hospital in Zambia. This message came out within a year or two of President Chiluba taking over from Kenneth Kaunda after an election. The following extracts illustrate the influence of British civil service training:-

"I expect a marked change not only in attitudes, but also in the carrying out of managerial functions from each and everyone of you".

"Now (the public) demand that all managers bring forth nothing but excellence in their Performance".

"People will .... Expect a service which is timely ..... from a well turned out officer, in smart offices, as opposed to now when one encounters a shabbily dressed officer with a snarling face in dusty offices with torn seats and curtains". "I have full confidence that all of you will take this message for the year 1994 with the seriousness it deserves".

While there is here a concern for discipline the message was very similar to the one delivered in Uganda in 1972 when Idi Amin took over a last outpost owned by Britain – what had been the Empire Cotton Growing Corporations Research Station at Namulonge. The main concern seemed to be that the golf course and lawns were well looked after!

Alan Coren's weekly send-ups of President Idi Amin's speeches in the magazine *Punch* were clever but, to those living in Uganda, inaccurate and unnecessarily offensive. Although he did several evil acts such as ordering the killing of Archbishop Luwum I don't believe Idi Amin had a long-term plan to become President. He was pushed into it by Milton Apolo Obote who left for the 1971 Commonwealth meeting with a warning that he must sort out various illegal gold and ivory transactions before he came back or face a trial. The fairly obvious response was to see that he didn't come back!

While some of Amin's sayings were silly or funny peculiar some were witty. They showed that, had he received a good education, he could have become a responsible leader. At Namulunge he produced a quick and witty response when warned they were approaching trees with low branches – "I'm used to taking cover!" His advice on birth control was sensible:-

"Whoever does not want children should restrict herself"[5]

In an address to Makerere students he had advice which could have reduced the spread of HIV/AIDS: "Many of you have gonorrhoea. This is not right. As future leaders of our nation you must have clean bodies". It is now accepted that infection with other STD's greatly increases the risk of HIV/AIDS infection.

Other witty but sensible Amin-isms include the following:-

"If you are drunk, for God's sake park your car and rest till you feel alright"

"Keep you compounds clean, slash the grass or it will grow into a big forest and invite snakes and rats".

Many people, including Ugandans, are confused about Amin When he died on August 16 2003 the obituaries were by no means totally negative. We had such relatively happy memories of his first 15 months in power that we sent a message to him in 1999. We were sailing up the Red Sea after 3 years in South Africa on an Italian cruise ship. When we got near Jeddah we threw a sealed bottle over the side. The message inside said "Are you missing Uganda as much as we are!" The Ugandan paper the *Sunday Monitor* carried a nostalgic editorial after his death. "It will be with definite sadness that a big section of the sporting fraternity will greet the news" due to his "unbelievable" support for Ugandan football. The British *Sunday Telegraph* commented that "he carried within his breast all the complexes of humiliated colonised people who both admire and hate those who rule them". Having met him during our 1971 Open Day for around 20 minutes my memory of him is on balance positive and of someone you could joke with. I do not agree with the British High Commissioner who is reported to have said of him that "he had just enough intelligence to know he couldn't run the country". In fact to speculate one could say that had he become a figurehead President with a decision making Prime Minister he could have survived – but for all the tribal scores that had to be settled in the Army. These later, of course, spilled over into the whole of Uganda.

When I guided Idi Amin around the three 2 ha small-holdings at the University Farm I briefly argued but didn't joke. According to Laura Merton[6] her father, when Amin's personal pilot, frequently joked with him and regularly beat him when racing in the Air Force swimming pool. However Denis Hills nearly lost his life when he joked about Amin as "the black Nero" in his book "The White Pumpkin". He was eventually saved by the intervention of the Queen and Mr. Callaghan – who flew out to collect him.

Recently Roy Clarke, a Britisher married to a Zambian, got into similar trouble in Lusaka when, in his column in the *Post* newspaper, he lampooned the government as being like animals in a Game Park. He was threatened with deportation.[7] In most African societies there are recognised "Joking Relationships" between different sexes and age groups. Our Kenyan adopted daughter Kageha comes from near Tiriki Location in Western Kenya. The American anthropologist Walter Sangree did a 2 year study[8] of the Tiriki people in the 1950's in which he describes joking relationships. With the current emphasis on sex education for AIDS prevention it is essential that the old systems of instruction by aunts, uncles and grand parents be revived. "Grandparents and grandchildren banter a great deal. Their joking is often sexually toned". But "these 2 categories ... would never be permitted to marry". Joking relationships occur throughout Africa and are a form of bonding between men and women as well as between men of different age groups.

One of the serious topics in the "Lighter Look" articles was HIV/AIDS. That may seem surprising and it might seem an insensitive subject for a westerner to tackle. However by the 1990's I had had some experience of AIDS Education in Zimbabwe, Zambia and Kenya. In Zambia we had a mixed team, including always a PWA (Person with AIDS), which spoke at secondary schools. I used to joke as we set out: "You can't teach about condoms if you don't wear your seat belt"! Once in the school hall the atmosphere was invariably jovial. A condom demonstration using a banana was hilarious but we invariably avoided doing this for the whole school.

Ours was a church hospital team whereas I have seen condoms demonstrated in government schools.

In a Harare school I once sat in on a talk with the theme "abstinence until marriage" given by a Scripture Union woman in her late 20's who claimed to be a virgin. Hopefully the message got across but soon afterwards I was asked in a primary school "Can we get AIDS from sharing a toothbrush?"[9] This amused me but I then found a Ministry of Education guide which showed "sex with many partners" next to "sharing a toothbrush" in a diagram of how HIV is spread. The theme of my Lighter Look was "the risks some people take". I used as an example Dervla Murphy's[10] story of hitch hikers who have sex with lorry drivers and consider it "all part of the African experience".

A second "Lighter Look" on AIDS took a look at the Sugar Mummy issue.[11] In Lusaka in the 1980's our by then teenage Kenyan daughter was waiting in the car while I went to the Central Post Office. A Zambian man approached the car and said to her in effect: "Why don't you leave that old sugar daddy and come with me!" She replied indignantly: "He's not my sugar daddy he's my real daddy!" Fortunately the man went on his way but looked extremely perplexed!

The sugar daddy issue came up when I joined a UNICEF funded team writing books on AIDS for secondary schools. For some strange reason I was assigned some of the sections covering delicate cultural issues. I was later told that it would be discriminatory to have sugar daddies without sugar mummies! The African sugar mummy is not as common a phenomenon as the sugar daddy where the trend towards younger and younger sexual partners has been fuelled by fears of contracting HIV. Furthermore, with no evidence to support it the claim was made, and apparently believed, that an HIV positive man can be cleansed of his infection by having sex with a virgin. One can only hope that the efforts to stamp out this completely false idea have been successful. Failure in this must greatly increase the rate of spread. It is important to note that although someone receiving anti-retroviral treatment is less likely to pass on their virus it is possible. Hopefully this aspect is covered in anti-retroviral counselling.

Uganda is held up as an example of how African countries should tackle the spread of HIV. One humourous Anti AIDS slogan which I had a slight connection with is: "Practice Zero Grazing". When Idi Amin in 1971 visited the 3 small holdings I was in charge of at the Makerere University Farm one of them involved zero grazing. I wrote in my Lighter Look[12]:- "Technically it means keeping your cow in a stall and carrying grass to it rather than allowing it to wander around looking for its own. Used in anti-AIDS campaigns the slogan refers more to the male of the species. Presumably the man is expected to stay at home with his wife (the cow) rather than looking around for greener pastures!" A year or two afterwards in the mid 90's there was an unfortunate incident at a Commonwealth Conference in New Zealand. A leading Kenyan politician was sent home after being accused of an indecent proposal in a hotel. When he was christened "The Bull of Auckland" by the Kenyan press and parliamentarians we were not sure whether Kenyans had got the zero grazing message!

In writing for African newspapers I was usually careful not to aim direct criticisms at the president or other highly influential politicians. An exception was an article I wrote in Zambia about the invasive and pernicious weed Lantana camara. It is a menace world wide because it smothers grassland and renders millions of hectares useless. From what we have seen in our 2003-4 visits to Kenya, South Africa and Zimbabwe it is still being planted as a hedge around schools. My article in Zambia mentioned that President Kaunda's State House had so much growing in its grounds that it could be seen over the 2 meter wall. The Editor cut out that sentence but I am certain this would not have led to my being sacked or deported. 'KK' was not that sort of president.

My wife and to a lesser extent myself interacted with President Kenneth Kaunda[13] over the years 1977-96. This leads us to conclude that he was probably one of the best of Africa's early independence dictators. He was very abstemious, a vegetarian, teetotaler and we have never seen any sign of the millions of dollars *Time* magazine accused him of salting away. He was an advocate of humanism but also had great respect and rapport with religious bodies. When the 1st of July 1990 attempted coup was overthrown by the Army his first action was to sing a hymn!

My first observation of him was at the Lusaka showground on World Food Day 1978. I was showing slides to a group of street boys when he appeared behind us. The security guards with him tried to shoe the boys away but KK told them to stay and he enjoyed watching the show with them. It showed me his essential humanity and sympathy with poorer Zambians.

Security at State House in the 1970's was fairly lax except for a period after Rhodesian forces crossed Lake Kariba and attacked Joshua Nkomo's house, next to President Kaunda's walled garden. On one occasion when in a government television vehicle I was told to take over as driver as otherwise there would be problems with security protocol at the State House gate! When Theresa left a paper she had written on mosquito breeding at the gate she was personally phoned by President Kaunda next day. Later a fellow Quaker was arrested for walking too often past State House. The British High Commissioner persuaded him to change his route and call for a cup of tea!

The print journalism often involved being an agricultural correspondent in the local newspaper. In Uganda from 1968-72 the *Uganda Argus* ran a weekly column which was also published by *Munno* – the national Uganda paper which had the best rural distribution through the Catholic church. With one article I produced not "a storm in a tea cup" but "a hurricane in the cabbage patch"! I had quoted a visiting Makerere Professor of Nutrition as claiming that Ugandans were getting poorer nutrition because they chose to eat cabbages rather than their traditional relishes and spinach. This led to a crisis when several individuals and institutions cancelled their regular cabbage orders!

The main cabbage producing area in Uganda was Kigezi District, a high and fertile area of hills and valleys. The German agency, GTZ, had a horticulturalist there promoting cabbage growing. Naturally the farmers were upset by having their market undermined by a newspaper columnist! A protest meeting was called and a telegram drafted to go to the Permanent Secretary in Entebbe! A telegram returned to GTZ asking the German cabbage expert to write a "defence of cabbages" – extolling their virtues and food value. My defence was that I had only quoted the Professor and actually concluded that both had a place. The main advantage of the cabbage was its transportability over 8 hours of hot tarmac and dusty, dirt roads. My other omission was that I failed to determine that my pseudonym in the Luganda paper *Munno-Agricola* – was the telegraphic address of the Permanent Secretary!

The Zambian "Lima Time" television farming programme started in 1982 as a result of a casual visit to the studios. Much of its success depended on Alfred Kalonga, the producer, and his great feel for farming with his Batonga background. He had received training whereas the rest of us were novices and tried to learn as we went along. There were some hilarious moments. The Minister of Agriculture agreed to launch it with an interview with me the presenter. He insisted on having the questions in advance and then came with his answers in writing. He fumbled the papers as he spoke but fortunately asked to see it before transmission. He cancelled it on the spot and we did a re-take with a prepared speech. I was then told that I should have known the Minister was incoherent after a good lunch!

There were continuous problems with getting a film team together for outdoor filming on farms. But we became adept at using the studio by bringing in potted weeds or equipment to demonstrate. When I tried to make a similar series in Zimbabwe in 1990 a free-lance video producer told me: "They will use you to the hilt, they will kick you in the teeth and you will get no thanks!" We managed to complete 10 programmes but eventually the enthusiasm waned when bosses changed. All the programmes were filmed outdoors and covered from Chiredzi to Lions Den, Mazvingo and Gutu. A popular programme was "Snakes and the Farmer" when I conducted an interview while standing a few inches from a Gaboon Viper! In Zambia we had had considerable snake experience when our son built up a collection in the garden. When taking a Land Rover full of snake boxes to the Teaching Hospital for a lecture on snake bites we arrived to find one box empty! We never found the occupant!

The Lima Time TV programme seemed justified once there were substantial numbers of people with sets – as there were in Zambia by the 1980's. Farmer viewers were however few and far between. Nowadays solar panels have made a set more feasible in remote areas. However about 1985 I did get a complaint from a farmer that 8.30 p.m. was too late for him as 8.00 p.m. was his bed time! We had considered 8.30 p.m. to be prime time for most Zambians – with the main ZBC news following at 9.00 p.m. This also had its problems as the programme and my voice would suddenly be cut off in mid sentence as the TV studio clock struck

9.00 p.m. Occasionally the rest of the programme was not transmitted after the news and the pictures and words of wisdom were
lost forever!

Being recognized as a TV presenter has great advantages for
feed back from the public. I would from time to time be approached
in Cairo Road – the main street of Lusaka. While we would have
welcomed more rural viewers we were anxious to inform all
Zambians about farming and hopefully encourage some to invest
in a farm or retire to a farm! One man asked if I would come and
film his excellent crop of tomatoes while another asked for the
address of where we filmed the programme on rabbits!

We had hints that members of the Cabinet and even Prersident
Kaunda watched some "Lima Times" from time to time. But the
real evidence for this came in 1994 when we lived at St. Francis
Hospital, Katete. "KK" was no longer President but came to the
hospital electioneering with a motley crowd of supporters. Theresa
spoke to him in the hospital and suggested he call on me at home.
I was typing on the dining table in our very small cottage when a
crowd came to our rickety gate. They seemed to be breaking it so
I came out gesticulating! To my surprise I came face to face with
a smiling former President! He then introduced me to the crowd
as the former presenter of Lima Time. He commented that when
I was around farming in Zambia was making progress. He did not
mention that he was in charge for 5 years after my contract ended!

Access to the President came up as an issue when our Dutch
cameraman, Werner Haas, and I made a series of programmes in
1985 in the Luangwa National Park. It was at the time of a seminar for all the senior staff of radio, print media and television in
Chichele Lodge. In a discussion session we expatriates were
accused of having direct access to "the leadership" – meaning
primarily "KK"! I made a strong rebuttal in which I said I was a
civil servant and had the same lack of access as they did. My only
access was either through State House or ministers televisions or
my wife! She, being in the university, was not restricted like we
were. Her intervention over mosquito breeding had already shown
she could make a direct approach. It should be pointed out that
"KK", like other Presidents, such as Banda, Nyerere and Seretse
Khama, had several expatriate State House advisers in the early
days of independence. This was obviously still a touchy issue with
senior civil servants.

111

Werner Haas, was still in Zambia in 1987 when I made a return visit to make a video programme for the charity Harvest Help. He agreed to join me as cameraman and editor. The programme was about the Gwembe Lakeshore Project along Lake Kariba. I had been involved with fellow Quakers, Leo[14] and Ginnie Goodfellow, since it started. Permission to make it was negotiated with the Minister of Agriculture, General Chinkuli, during a visit to London – but wires got crossed. In the middle of editing the tapes we had shot, our studio was invaded and the half edited tapes confiscated! The authorities were touchy because of foreign camera crews making videos on AIDS illegally and they said they wanted to check. They claimed we did not have proper authorization. That evening I contacted General Chinkuli who asked me to meet him next morning, a Saturday, in his office. He had extracted the tapes from the Permanent Secretary's office and gave them to me with instructions to leave the same day for London – with the tapes! It all seemed rather clandestine but was in a good cause!

Our main means of light relief, while in Africa, came from the BBC World Service and its regular use of BBC comedies like Hancock's Half Hour and Much Binding in the Marsh. During the 1970's war with Rhodesia, while we were living near Lusaka, the BBC was augmented by almost nightly repeats on Rhodesian Radio of the same comedies – designed to entertain the troops along the border. It was a traumatic time particularly when a Presidential order was made for a curfew and black out from 8.00 p.m. each evening. Our garden worker was returned to his hut by soldiers wielding rifles with bayonets when trying to reach his long drop toilet! We found the blackout particularly tedious after the authorities ordered a complete switch off of electricity at 8.00 p.m. A bit of Hancock was just what we needed. The irony was that when the air raids started they all took place in broad daylight!

Although the BBC World Service was not much listened to by Africans the BBC African Service has had an extensive African following right up to the present time. It is one of the best things that Britain has done for Africa. When I spent several weeks in a Kampala Hotel in 1975, with OAU delegates trying to sort out Angola, one could hear them tuning in to the BBC News. But humour goes very much with nationality and few would have found Much Binding in the Marsh amusing – or understood the jokes!

A recent trend that hopefully will be followed in Africa is the re-writing of British comedies for other audiences. It has been done in Nairobi with a Ki-Swahili version of the farming programme "The Archers". Recently there is a move to produce Indian versions of "Yes, Minister" and "Keeping up Appearances". The Hindi language translation of this is "The crow who tries to walk like a peacock"! "Birds of a Feather" has apparently been made with a Zimbabwean theme – "Robert Mugabe is a sex God".[15] The story is of two overweight matrons who are enjoying the fruits following the arrest of their husbands for insulting the President. It will be some time before it can be shown in Harare! Africa will have made great progress when its leaders can be laughed at without the makers of programmes such as "Yes, Prime Minister" being arrested.

The nearest we came across to the ridiculing of politicians by African journalists was the column in *The Times* of Zambia by Kapelwa Musonda. In one column in the 1980's he had a complete take-off of a state visit by President Kamuzu Banda to Lusaka. He employed the flowery speeches used on such occasions to make a complete farce of the event. British politicians, although they must squirm at some Yes, Minister programmes probably also welcome getting known intimately by the public. Hopefully African states will soon feel strong enough as in India to poke fun at their politicians with Yes, Minister style television programmes.

In conclusion I am grateful to have shared in a small way some joking relationships with African colleagues. A sense of humour and the ability to laugh at oneself are tremendous assets in all societies. From our experiences over 50 years there are many Africans who can laugh at themselves. One feels such people will pull through the difficulties of the future.

NOTES

1. Doris Lessing, African Laughter, Harper Collins, 1992, London.
2. The Chronicle, Bulawayo, Oct. 16 1992.
3. Lenny Henry, a biography by Jonathan Margolos, 1995, Orion, London.
4. Letter to the Traffic Manager, Uganda Railway, Nairobi from the Station Master at Londiani, 1903: from Pioneers Scrapbook – reminiscences of Kenya 1890-1968. Edited by Elspeth Huxley and Arnold Curtis, Evans, London, 1980.

5. Voice of Uganda, 11 Jan. 1974.
6. Daily Telegraph, 19 August 2003.
7. Times of Zambia, 27 April 2004.
8. Walter Sangree. Age, Prayer and Politics in Tiriki, Kenya. Oxford University Press, 1966, London, page 31.
9. The Herald, Harare, Zimbabwe, 29th April 1992.
10. Dervla Murphy, "The Ukimwi Road: From Kenya to Zimbabwe", 1990.
11. The Herald, 5th September 1992.
12. The Herald, Harare, 5th Sep. 1992.
13. After KK's loss of the presidency in the 1991 election and the take over by Frederick Chiluba my wife and I flew from Harare to visit him in the small colonial house he was allocated in Kabulonga. One aim was to encourage him in his peace making initiatives.
14. Leo Goodfellow died on 8th Otober 1994 while testing a friend's microlight. Ginnie, a brilliant horticulturalist, still lives at Munyama on the lake.
15. The Times, London. 14th February 2003, Media Editor.

CHAPTER VIII

The Struggle and Life Under Majority Rule

A PRE-OCCUPATION for the United Nations, the Commonwealth and in particular for African countries after the end of the Second World War was the struggle against racial discrimination. The Afrikaans word Apartheid – meaning the state of being apart – became known world-wide in 1948. This was after the National Party (NP) won the first post-war election in South Africa. While "The Struggle" refers predominantly to the campaign to replace Apartheid in South Africa, similar discrimination and loss of rights took place to some degree in the Rhodesias and Kenya. An error or slip in Nelson Mandela's autobiography credits the Afrikaner nationalists as having won the Anglo-Boer War.[1] If they had the Apartheid policy would certainly have been introduced before 1948 – and there would never have been a Communist MP in the Cape Town parliament – elected by a very restricted electorate of black, mixed race and Asian voters. Sam Kahn, who stayed with us in Serowe, Bechuanaland to escape the post Sharpeville arrests and get to Ghana, served as an MP from 1948 until 1952, when he was expelled. He is remembered for his speech on the Mixed Marriages Act which he described as "the immoral offspring of an illicit union between racial superstition and biological ignorance"! He went on to claim that it incorporated "pseudo-biological phantasies about race purity".

In 1988 when lecturing in South Africa I was encouraged by the Institute of Race Relations in Johannesburg to call on Methodist Bishop Rev. Stanley Mogoba. When I mentioned Sam Kahn his face lit up. "We worshipped that man when I was at school", he said. He considered him to be a major voice of African opinion in the 1940's because his speeches in parliament were usually to be found in the newspapers. Stanley later became very active in the Pan African Congress (PAC) during the 1990's. He was elected National President in December 1996 and won a landslide victory in April 2000 to retain the position. The PAC under his leadership has not presented as powerful a challenge to the Government as expected.

Mandela's autobiography brings out the importance of the Sharpeville Massacre on 21st March 1960. Although the firing of over 700 shots was directed at a Pan African Congress rally, in which 69 people were killed, it provided an opportunity for mobilizing the whole country in the struggle to overthrow the Apartheid Government. A month before Harold Macmillan, the British Prime Minister, had made his "winds of change" speech. He acknowledges (page 226) that his party, the African National Congress, used the Sharpeville Massacre to mobilize the country. The Government declared a State of Emergency on 30 March, suspended habeas corpus and made arrests all over the country. A small number escaped over the border to Swaziland and one section of this group were air lifted to Serowe in what is now Botswana. They included the former Communist MP Sam Kahn, the wife of Oliver Tambo, who was trying to join her husband in London, Patrick van Rensburg, the ex-South African diplomat, and Isaac (Billy) Modise, later High Commissioner to Canada. There were 15 others in the party selected for evacuation via Serowe.

It was during 1989 that Oliver Tambo, then President of the African National Congress in exile, was taken seriously ill. We wrote to express our concern to Adelaide, his wife, in London and offered the use of our Welsh farmhouse for his recuperation. Some months later, when we had moved to the University of Zimbabwe, a letter was forwarded from Oliver himself. He thanked us and said he would like to take up the offer. Sadly we failed to find someone to offer an alternative place for him as the house already had tenants. A few months later on July 18 1990 I was travelling on the same flight from Harare to Johannesburg as Nelson Mandela on his first return to South Africa as a free man after his tour of ANC bases and offices. During the flight he moved to tourist class to talk to ANC people in front of me and was mobbed by children wanting his autograph. Sadly Oliver died from another stroke two weeks after the assassination of Chris Hani in 1993 and before the historic "one person one vote" election on 27 April 1994.

To extract the post-Sharpeville refugees from Swaziland in 1960 a plan was developed to fly them from Francistown airport to Ghana using a Ghana Airways DC 3. My role in this was approved by the District Commissioner, Serowe. The main organizer was George Clay, an *Observer* (London) journalist who had links with Canon Collins of the Defence and Aid Fund in London. He brought from Pretoria a supply of aviation fuel for the small plane that made 4 trips from Swaziland to the bush air strip outside Serowe. Our role was to accommodate 3 people, arrange for others to stay in private homes and then provide transport to Francistown airport. Since this was operated by the Witwatersrand Native Labour Association (WENELA) the pick up was timed for dawn on the 12th September 1960. I was warned to move away before take off because the airport staff were mainly South Africans.[2] A previous airlift was aborted when drums of fuel were placed on the runway.

According to a report by Mr. T.F. Betts to the Bechuanaland Administration my role was "in a voluntary capacity" to act as "a link ..... between the Christian Action Defence and Aid Fund and the South African United Front in Dar-es-Salaam". I "advanced funds on reimbursement to political refugees in transit who had been approved by the SAUF".[3] However over the next year we also assisted refugees from South West Africa and the Pan African Congress (PAC). One of our visitors, over the 6th to 8th May 1961, although not officially a refugee, was Patrick Duncan. We knew him because in 1959 I reported on Bechuanaland affairs in his Liberal Party magazine, *Contact.* He had recently defected to the PAC and was looking for a farm as an external base. It seemed possible that it would be used for sabotage activities in South Africa. I took him to see Theresa who had been seriously ill and was recovering in Serowe Hospital. We had a heated exchange over whether "The Struggle" had to become violent to succeed in overthrowing Apartheid. This was only a few months before we moved north to work in Kenya, and later Uganda, for 10 years.

Our move led to a major lull in our involvement. Interest was kept alive by people like Hannah Stanton who was in effect a refugee from Apartheid while on the staff of Makerere University. Like many Christians that had been forced to leave South Africa she had been active at several levels in "The Struggle". When we left Uganda in 1972 and travelled by boat via Cape Town I picked up a copy of the *Cape Times* on 17 April 1972. A short article on a report by The Christian Institute showed that "more than 100 clergymen .... had had action taken against them by the Government since 1957". The visit to Cape Town exposed us to petty Apartheid because of our adopted Kenyan daughter, Kageha. In one incident we were told we could not be served with tea in an open-air café outside Parliament. We got round this by serving ourselves with ice creams! In the other incident a bus conductor tried to split our family by making 4 of us go downstairs. The driver intervened with the explanation: "These people are foreigners and don't understand our funny laws! Let them stay where they are". For the rest of our visit and in Durban the Quakers looked after us.

Our move to East Africa was partly motivated by a feeling that we would eventually get sucked into a more violent confrontation. Since 1960 there have been so many violent confrontation areas in Africa that we have preferred to work in areas where we would be able to do useful work without living behind barbed wire and electric fences. This may seem like running away from difficult situations but is one of the advantages of being an expatriate rather than a settler as discussed in an earlier chapter. Nadine Gordimer in a 1994 lecture she gave in the USA mentioned that in the 1960's, although she had sympathies with the "The Struggle" she did not make any formal commitment. Having a non-political family she felt revolution was something for the black people to undertake. Fortunately she and other white South Africans did not continue with that attitude so that Joe and Ruth Slovo, Sam Kahn, Solly Sachs, Bram Fischer and many Asians including the Meers prevented "The Struggle" from being an all-black affair on the ANC side.[4] In Zimbabwe, although people like Guy Clutton-Brock and Quakers Stanley and Margaret Moore made important early contributions, The Struggle was much more of an all-black movement. Guy is at the time of writing the only white Zimbabwean to be commemorated in Harare's Heroes Acre. Sir Garfield Todd and his daughter Judith, although much praised for supporting "The struggle" both lost their citizenship and right to vote in 2000. They were accused of supporting the opposition party the Movement for Multi-Party Democracy (MMD). Quakers have tried to make positive contributions and were exercised about the issue of sanctions against South Africa. The majority of South African Quakers probably opposed them. In Britain a compromise was reached in supporting limited sanctions. Sports sanctions on cricket and rugby were highly effective because the white South African population is so dominated by sport. When we joined the Mtunzini Sports Club in KwaZulu-Natal in 1996, in order to play tennis and squash, we couldn't escape this impression.

The sports sanction policy was originally organized by Peter Hain, now a leading Labour politician and member of the British cabinet. He had excellent Pan-African credentials having been born in Nairobi and brought up in South Africa in a family that were forced to leave because of their political activities. His mother was banned in 1963 and his father in 1964. They left for London in 1966 when Peter was aged 16 and a pupil at the Pretoria Boys' High School. There is no doubt that sports sanctions played an important role in swinging certain whites behind the ending of Apartheid. I was not convinced that an academic boycott would be effective and think a close study will show that it delayed new thinking among academic Afrikaners.

From 1950-54 at Reading University, and afterwards at the University of London, I had several West African friends who were highly political and supporters of "the struggle" against colonial rule and race discrimination. Although we hadn't yet met, Theresa and I were both involved in the Africa Bureau. To quote John Gunther:[5] London in the 1950's "has any number of organizations, white, black and mixed, devoted ...... to anti-imperialist causes". "In London, the most imperial of cities, one may find Englishmen ..... like the Rev. Michael Scott – devoting their lives to the cause of African liberation". We were both infected with the idea of doing what we could for "the cause" – or "The Struggle".

In Nigeria during the Mid 1950's I was immersed in agriculture but regularly read the Observer newspaper from London. Colin Legum was remarkable for his coverage of Africa and, as an exile, was particularly well informed about South Africa. His articles informed me not only about South Africa but also about what was then Southern Rhodesia.

During my Colonial Service leave in Britain during 1956 I studied for one term down the road from my mother at the Quaker

College, Woodbrooke, in Birmingham. Fellow students included a Nigerian and a South African, Yolisa Bokwe, from near Fort Hare. With a Christmas book token I bought the just published book "Naught for your Comfort" by Trevor Huddleston. By the time I started my post-"retirement" tour of Africa in January 1958 Huddleston had already returned to Britain. However I wrote to Father Jarrett Kerr of the Community of the Resurrection and was invited to stay there when I got to Johannesburg. The visit exposed me to many of the evils of Apartheid, in particular the removal of non-whites in Sophiatown to make way for the white suburb of Triompf. I wandered round the half destroyed township with its signs of "we won't move" and young men attempting to play golf on the wasteland around the boundary.[6]

Before setting out on my 1958 tour I spent Christmas with Walter and Maisie Birmingham at Legon University, Accra in the newly independent Ghana. It gave me a feel for what obviously excited Nelson Mandela at the time when he counted 17 former colonies that were scheduled to become independent states (Long Walk to Freedom, page 224) within the next few years. Passing through Lagos to join the M/S *General Mangin* en route for Pointe Noire I met Ezekial Mphahlele who was teaching at Lagos Grammar School as a South African exile. In his autobiography[7] Alan Paton, a leading South African Liberal, describes how later that year an All-Africa People's Conference was held in Accra. Ezekiel wanted to launch a "bitter attack on Liberals" presumably for being too soft on Apartheid. The Algerians were at the time fighting France and resented the idea of a non-violent revolution which the Conference proposed. A rider was added to give support to those obliged to retaliate for violent exploitation.

My 1958 journey to South Africa by rail, bus, small plane and boat took 2 months and I passed through Belgian and French colonies that would receive independence within a few years. The Belgian Congo, renamed Zaire, would be plunged into violence by the time our Sharpeville refugees landed in Leopoldville on their way to Ghana. Sam Kahn wrote to describe their reception on 14 September 1960, 2½ months after independence had been declared. The troops at the airport were clearly under Belgian control following the mutiny in the Thysville barracks on 5th July 1960. Their main concern was that the soldiers guarding them "kept dropping off to sleep as they stood and we were in some terror that the loaded rifle might fall to the ground and …. accidently trigger off a shot".[8]

Others involved in "The Struggle" at this stage included the pilot Hebert Bartaune of Bulawayo. I had a long chat with him on the phone in 1990 when he was retired in Walvis Bay. He considered himself a taxi driver and said taxi drivers "don't ask the business of their clients". Earlier in the 1960's he flew Nelson Mandela to Dar-es-Salaam and all the Rhodesian prime ministers including Lord Malvern, Ian Smith and Garfield Todd. In 1960-61 he also flew Dag Hammarskjold Director-General of the United Nations. Dag's body was found 11km north-west of Ndola in Zambia on 18 September 1961 near the burnt out wreckage of his UN plane. The cause of the crash remains a mystery but the fighting for the secession of Katanga continued until 15 January 1963. George Clay, who organised the DC3 Ghana Airways flight with Oliver Tambo in London and brought fuel in Pretoria for the small planes, died in another 1960's Zaire battle when caught in cross-fire while covering the fighting for London newspapers.

Although in 1959 Bechauanaland was somewhat of a backwater as regards political activity[9] we were exposed to South African issues soon after we arrived. Motsamai Mpho and Z.K. Mathews were both in the 1956 Treason Trial and came from Bechuanaland. We enjoyed visits to the Mpho's open air kitchen in Palapye and once had a chat with Prof. Z.K. Mathews, Principal of Fort Hare, at an agricultural show. He later deserted South Africa, where he made a deep impression on Nelson Mandela (pages 46-47), and became an ambassador for Botswana. In Serowe itself Peter Boerman, a black South African, was having problems with some of the white trading community, often visited us with his family.

Uganda was an interesting step on my 1958 travels and had a South African element. I visited Noni Jabavu (aged 84 at the time of writing), the author, a daughter of the late Professor Davidson Jabavu of Fort Hare. He was the first black professor in 1916 and President of the All African Convention. In January 2004 Noni was present at the family house near Middledrift in the Eastern Cape when it was declared a national monument. In 1958 Noni was living in Kampala and was married to a distant relative of mine, Michael Crosfield. Her book "The Ochre People"[10] is still popular and gives a highly evocative and amusing insight into life in what is now the Eastern Cape. Her second book 'Drawn in Colour' was written during her 5 years in Uganda and shows some attitudes which developed in England when she was educated at the Quaker girls' school, The Mount. While in Johannesburg in 1958 I was taken to see the area of Soweto named after Noni's grandfather John Tengo Jabavu who, after the Boer War, led a delegation to the British parliament to protest against the projected Union of South Africa. George Cadbury, Michael's grandfather, was then a leading Liberal politician. During the Boer War he earned the title "Pro-Boer" from Afrikaners although his stance was actually more neutral. As a Quaker, he was totally against all wars.

The next stop on my 1958 tour was to visit Nairobi and Quaker friends who were working in Mwea-Tebere with some of the Kikuyu people detained during the Mau Mau rebellion. The emergency was coming to an end and on March 10th 1957 8 Africans had been elected to the Legislative Council under the Lyttelton Constitution. Kenya was well on the way to independence which came on December 12 1963 and accelerated education programmes led to British Quakers being asked to supplement the work of the Americans who started the Friends Africa Mission in 1902. Walter Martin, who had studied with me on the same course in London in 1953-54 represented the Friends Service Council in Nairobi. On June 2 1961 he was in a Quaker delegation that visited Jomo Kenyatta and other detainees in Maralal. Jomo was released soon afterwards in August 1961 following "very cordial discussions"[11] with the Governor, Sir Evelyn Baring.

From Kenya I moved south by bus, boat and train to what was then Southern Rhodesia. My first stop was at St Faiths Mission, Rusape at the home of Guy and Molly Clutton-Brock. This was at the time a place where nationalists met and planned "The Struggle". I have a tattered copy of the first 2 pages of a "Statement of Principles, Policy and Programme" of the Southern Rhodesia African National Congress" dated 1957.[12] According to Robert Gabriel Mugabe[13] in a short section of the book to celebrate Guy's 80th birthday it was written by George Nyandoro, Robert Chikerema and Paul Mushonga with Clutton-Brock's help. He entitled his tribute to Guy "An Inspiration for Reconciliation". Guy died in Britain on the 29th January 1995 aged 89 and a tree was

122

planted in the Harare Heroes Acre. We visited Molly in a nursing home near Mold in North Wales recently (April 2004). The time in the 1980's when Robert Mugabe made visits to North Wales from meetings in London seems very distant now. But there is still a great need for reconciliation.

My 1958 travels took me by train to Salisbury where I called on Herbert Chitepo, one of the founders of Zimbabwe's Struggle. He was then an advocate in chambers run by a European firm. In August 1963 he was appointed Chairman of the Zimbabwe African National Union. He had already been persuaded by the party to go into voluntary exile in May 1962. He was Tanganyika's first African Director of Public Prosecutions but resigned and moved to Zambia in 1966. He was assassinated in a car bomb attack on 18th March 1975 outside his house south of Lusaka. His death remains one of the mysteries of "The Struggle". A 140 page book on the incident has recently been published in the USA.[14] Four people have confessed to the killing and countless others have been accused. He was a towering figure who, like Josiah Tongogara, could have played an invaluable role in stabilising Zimbabwe. Josiah died in a car accident on the eve of Independence in 1980, was buried in Mozambique and in 1982 re-buried in Heroes Acre. On one of our visits to Harare in the early 80's we asked our taxi driver what happened to him as we were being driven along Tongogara Avenue. He was only 40 when he died and we had not heard of the accident. The taxi driver replied that "only Mr. Mugabe knows".

There is a delightful story of an informal meeting between Ian Smith and Josiah Tongogara in 1979. Both were delegates to the 1979 Lancaster House Conference and were negotiators in the cease-fire which preceded Independence. Both came from the same area of The Midlands and indeed Josiah greeted Smith with a smile and reminded him that Mrs. Smith Senior used to give him sweets in the farm shop. I reminded Ian Smith of the meeting when we met in 1997 during his promotional tour of South Africa for the book "The Great Betrayal". A telling point in his promotional tour was that, when he handed over power in 1980, the Zimbabwe dollar was worth £1.02. On our most recent visit to Zimbabwe we took our Beverley Building Society savings account book to get it updated and closed. The 2003 balance of 500 dollars was just enough to buy a highly subsidised copy of the government paper,

The Chronicle. Ian Smith's defence of the 30,000 black and 6000 white deaths in the war was less convincing. But his face lit up when I mentioned Josiah Tongogara. He said: "If he had lived things might have gone much better".

Mugabe's training of the Fifth Brigade, using North Korean trainers, seems to have been an attempt to nullify any challenge to his power from Joshua Nkomo and his followers in Matabeleland. Some put the death toll higher than in "The Struggle for Independence". The tragedy of Zimbabwe is that the country started Independence with an embittered leader. The reconciliation he propounded was in retrospect tactical to prevent a flight of capital. In contrast, South Africa, perhaps partly because there was much less open warfare, had a leader who had learnt respect for his opponents. In 1982 I flew from Lusaka in Zambia to Francistown in Botswana in order to buy a Toyoto-Corolla car. I planned to return through newly independent Zimbabwe and visit a Quaker family. They were Derek and Edith Archer, who we had stayed with in 1980 just before the pre-independence election when Mugabe and ZANU/PF won. Derek had seen his future as a local government employee was limited and they bought The London Store in Juliasdale, high in the Eastern Highlands. On arrival they warned me to be careful about walking in the area because they were next to the Fifth Brigade barracks and their North Korean trainers. It was a forewarning of the suppression of Matabeleland which started within months of my visit. In one sense the North Korean involvement was a hangover from the Cold War. Freedom fighters from Rhodesia, South Africa, Mozambique and Angola were trained in the USSR, Korea and China. Some of the training was on Marxist lines which never seemed to cut much ice in Africa. On one 1970's Aeroflot flight London-Moscow-Budapest-Luanda-Lusaka I struck up a conversation with Nathan Shamuyarira, who was still in Robert Mugabe's cabinet in 2004. He commented cynically as we gazed at the heaps of rubbish and abandoned crates on Luanda's air port:- "Even if you've had a revolution you should be able to buy some brooms!" At one time in the 1990's he was reported to be trying to retire from politics but must have found that too difficult.

Back in 1958 I took the train from Salisbury to South Africa following the old route developed by Cecil Rhodes through

Bulawayo to Francistown. In retrospect it is fortunate that Cecil Rhodes and his successors didn't know about the potential for mining otherwise they would have made even more strenuous efforts to get Bechuanaland incorporated in the Union of South Africa. A year and half later in 1959 I was married and back in Serowe, 30 miles from the railway as Tribal Agricultural Officer to the Bamangwato Tribal Administration. About the same time the Rhodesian Selection Trust discovered copper and nickel near a mission hospital we used to visit called Madinare. The discovery of diamonds at Orapa about 10 years later and the wise economic policies of Seretse Khama and his government led to what is often considered to be Africa's most successful transition to independent status. Seretse took a strong but pacifist line with his neighbour South Africa and for many years had no army. His attitude to dialogue was that it had to be on a basis of human equality. He rejected the status quo in South Africa and declined overtures designed to blunt international pressure for change. When we returned on visits from Zambia in the 1970's we met a group of South African refugees at the Kagisong Refugee Centre set up by British Quakers in Gaborone. The same centre was also used for refugees from the fighting in Matabeleland, Zimbabwe in the 1980's.

Our earlier involvement in the struggle over Rhodesia was while we lived in Zambia. Most of this was the result of Quaker initiatives from London to maintain contacts between the warring parties – ZANU in Maputo, ZAPU in Lusaka and Ian Smith's Government in Salisbury. A Quaker mediation team, which involved Welshman, Walter Martin, ex UN official, Tony Gilpin and Trevor Jepson circulated once a year between those capitals. We hosted them in Lusaka between 1977 and 1979 and kept up a supply of footballs and teaching materials to some of the ZAPU youth camps west of Lusaka. This followed a visit to a camp where we found several 100 youths staring at us from behind trees. We were told they had nothing to do and it was then explained that this was "holiday time". Providing sports equipment and magazines was a modest response. I called regularly at the ZAPU offices in Lusaka and delivered these to Edward Ndlovu, later, after 1980, an M.P. for Matabeleland South. I chatted to him when invited to Parliament in 1982 by Didymus Mutasa, then the Speaker, and a great admirer of our friends the Clutton-Brocks. Since the deterioration in the economy in the 2000's he became a vociferous Mugabe supporter.

A tragic casualty of the Struggle for Zimbabwe was the UCZ[15] Quaker attender, Muriel Bissell, a Zambian of Canadian descent. She had responded to President Kaunda's 'Back to the Land' call and in 1969 bought a 52 acre farm in Lusaka West. Muriel Dorothy Bissell was remarkable for her strong stand on principles and her loyalty to her chosen nation. She was born in 1913 "into a wealthy family" and had a life-long ambition to serve in Africa. Until her mother's death in the early 1960's she couldn't achieve her ambition. She then applied to work for the United Church of Canada and from 1964 taught at the Mindolo Ecomenical Foundation in Kitwe. She frequently attended Quaker meetings in Lusaka and we sometimes came to her farm. This happened during one of the visits of the Quaker team. She was questioned about "these white men" by the freedom fighters in the ZIPRA[16] camp which Joshua Nkomo's ZAPU[17] had just set up next to her farm. When camps in the area were bombed in November 1978 she "disappeared" and was later found dead in her septic tank. Her manager, Richard Tembo, who she treated almost as a member of her family, was charged with her murder, convicted and executed on January 27 1989 in the Maximum Security Prison outside Kabwe.[18]

Richard sent a note to us before his execution through the local Catholic priest Father Frank McAuliffe of Saint Augustine Major Seminary, Kabwe. The Father wrote to us that "He did not seem in the least bit afraid of death and was singing and praying right up to the very end". There is still confusion over how he was involved in the murder of his employer or what the motive was. However that the incident had strong connections with "The Struggle" and the camp next door is undoubted. According to the *Canadian Globe* and *Mail* of November 21 1978[19] trouble started in the area after a raid by "helicopter-borne Rhodesian troops on Nov 2. Since the attacks numerous white farmers in the area have been harassed and held by guerillas" ..... "looking for Rhodesian fifth columnists" ..... An "Australian was hung by his feet and bayoneted. A group of armed men took over Miss Bissell's farm on Nov. 6". The report indicated that her friends who called on her "were shot at". Guerillas who were listed as witnesses in the trial never gave testimony and it seems were dropped once Richard Tembo made a confession. A co-accused, Brown Kacholola was acquitted because of lack of evidence.

Stephen Lewis, who later became a leading Canadian politician, used Muriel's death in an article entitled "Untainted by colonial guilt Canada should take time to understand" (*Toronto Star* Nov. 22 1978). He wrote:- "She took out Zambian citizenship, a devoted Quaker pacifist who loved the country and its President, Kenneth Kaunda. It's one of the horrible ironies of racial conflict that when the bloodbath starts, decency and pedigree mean nothing". He went on to compare her death to that of 2 white nuns killed in South Africa after the Sharpeville massacre "although they had worked their entire lives in the black shantytowns". A close friend of Muriel's since the 1930's wrote (letter dated 16/12/78) that if it was a question of choice "she might have chosen to live her Zambian days the same way again, even if it meant the same end". "Many of us talk, while Muriel lived her faith".

Much of the Lusaka West area was a no-go area during late 1978 and early 1979. One school holiday from England our son Jeremy, then aged 12, spent time with a Nigerian vet friend of ours, Chris Oparacha, visiting commercial farms. They had just performed some pig castrations with Chris's South African black assistant and their clothes were covered in blood. As they returned to town they were stopped at a ZIPRA road block. The freedom fighters ordered them out and questioned them and said they looked very suspicious. Fortunately Chris's power of persuasion saw them through. On another day I heard loud bangs when teaching and asked in the staff room whether it was bombs. I was told "No – it's some dynamiting in the quarry". On going to the Ministry of Education in the afternoon I saw crowds at every intersection and was told about that morning's raids on ZIPRA camps. I went straight to the University Teaching Hospital and found Theresa busy tending some of the several hundred wounded. The only contribution I could make was to offer some blood. I found the blood transfusion collecting centre almost deserted but managed to stir them into action. That evening Zambian television carried an urgent appeal for blood.

Teaching at the Natural Resources Development College on the edge of Lusaka from 1977 to 1982 meant regular contact with South African exiles on the staff. Several became good friends and

I particularly remember Mr. Ncube who was asked to move to head the ANC Secondary School in Tanzania. After we moved to Mount Makulu Research Station from 1982-86 these contacts diminished. Throughout the 1970's and 1980's there were times when what I would call Spymania occurred. During one period a fellow Quaker and government official who liked walking with an African friend in the Lusaka streets for exercise was "arrested" by men from "The Liberation Centre" which housed freedom fighters from Zimbabwe, Namibia and South Africa. They were beaten and interrogated and he was left lying semi-comatose under a bench until a more senior official arrived and got him to the UTH for treatment of his black eye, cuts and various bruises. The Zambian authorities could have done more to control such unprovoked violence and the lawlessness in Lusaka West.

After 1980 attention of course switched to SWAPO and the ANC following Independence in Zimbabwe. We had a letter from David J. Richie of Moorestown, New Jersey in the USA requesting to visit Afrikaners. He was well known in Quaker, pacifist and in particular work camping circles. David was puzzled as to why Afrikaans speaking people had such a hang-up about black people. He applied for a South African visa with something on those lines as his objective. He was refused a South African visa but felt a second choice would be to visit Afrikaners in Zambia. He stayed 3 days in February 1983 and came to our annual gathering of Zambian Quakers. We took him around the area where we lived at Chilanga to meet Afrikaner farmers. One in particular, Mr. Scholtz Nel, lived near the Police Training College, Lilayi and made a strong impression. He held quite firmly to South African Afrikaners beliefs but kept them largely to himself. His farm had an aura of invincibility and was rarely visited by Zambians without a major reason to do so. David Richie hopefully came away feeling he had a better understanding for South Africa's problems.

Some Afrikaner characteristics are very similar to those of other White South Africans and Rhodesians. Fay Chung, an education minister in President Mugabe's government, wrote to *The Financial Gazette*, a Harare weekly on the 7th December 1990 about the positive aspects of "Rhodesian culture". These were: "pioneering spirit, initiative, self reliance, love of nature and nationalism". If she had stayed in Zimbabwe later in the 1990's she could have had some stabilising influence on the regime. In practice she moved to the USA to work for the United Nations. From 2000 the situation was so polarised it would not have been possible for a member of the government to have made such a remark.

My own small attempt to make a contribution to "The Struggle" came as a response to the call by the Anti-Apartheid Movement for sports, economic and "cultural sanctions". The first two I had little problem with. Sports is so dominant an interest amongst the white community that it must have had a major effect, particularly in the case of cricket and rugby. Economic sanctions could also have a major impact on government and had been the main factor in the collapse of Ian Smith's regime. However I felt cultural sanctions, if they just cut people off from the rest of the world, were not likely to have a major effect and might do the opposite of what was intended. They led to some ridiculous situations. When I visited the University of Wisconsin, Madison in 1988 a South African born professor refused to meet me because I was going to visit South Africa. Just buying a ticket was enough to put me in isolation. In Kenya a US elephant trainer had to remove some African elephants he had trained when it was discovered they were born in the Kruger National Park! The Anglican/Quaker comedian, Donald Swann, had to fight off objections to his visiting South Africa to perform before multi-racial audiences. Prior to one of my tours I did have a supportive letter from the late Donald Woods, biographer and friend of Steve Biko.

The visits I made from 1980 onwards to South Africa were prompted by an invitation from the South African Institute of International Affairs (SAIIA) in Johannesburg. The main series of talks to groups of Institute members were entitled:- "Adjustment of whites to black rule in East and West Africa".[20] The invitation was extended through a fellow Quaker – H.W. van der Merwe. He has been described in the Foreword to his book[21] by Nelson Mandela as "contributing in no small way to the liberation of our country. It is because South Africa had people like H.W. van der Merwe that we were able to enjoy a dramatic and peaceful transition to democracy, which serves as an inspiration to the world". H.W. had mentioned the need for South Africans to know about life under majority rule at a Quaker gathering in Botswana in 1979. The suggestion for my talks had gone to various universities in

South Africa but we only got one favourable response – from The Rector of the Rand Afrikaans University in Johannesburg. They however referred it to the SAIIA. The reasoning behind the subject was that the main factor preventing an election on one-man one vote lines was white fears of black rule. I hoped to show that accounts in the media were often exaggerated and distorted. The fact that I and my family had lived under majority rule since the 1960's would hopefully dispel some of the fears.

My 15 or so talks[22] were delivered over the next 8 years to groups around South Africa and so coincided with what in Zimbabwe was called – "The Chicken Run" – the exodus of white people after Robert Mugabe won the 1980 and 1985 elections. Most of my audiences were white and I was startled to be sent to the University of Transkei in Umtata. At the airport the authorities demanded a Transkei visa but this was eventually waived. The almost entirely black audience were somewhat bemused by my subject. One student asked, quite reasonably, whether: "a white could be elected president by an all-black electorate?" I replied that it was extremely unlikely for many years but was not impossible. I quoted the recent cases of the Leakey brothers in Kenya. Philip had just been elected in the Langata constituency by almost entirely black voters. Richard was confidant of Arap Moi and later made Head of the Wildlife Service. My talk pointed out various pitfalls and stated that liberation and independence "has been disappointing for people of European origin as well as for the local African

An example of distorted news causing unnecessary alarm in South Africa was from the *London Sunday Telegraph* in 1978. Their reporter described a visit to the Victoria Falls on the Rhodesian side. The reporter was surprised on coming round an island to find nearly everyone in the Zambian boat was white! I was able to confirm that they were not East German or Russian communists as the reporter indicated! Most expatriates in Zambia were British – on generous topped up salaries from Britain.

On several occasions we flew Aeroflot to or from London, changing planes in Moscow, partly because it was cheaper but there must have been very few Russians and East Germans in Zambia in those days. Tourists were almost entirely local or from western countries. President Ceaucescu of Romania made a state visit on one occasion and went to the Victoria Falls to peer at the Rhodesian

130

soldiers through binoculars. Next day tourists could return and when we asked what were the railway engine noises at night we were told they were taking goods to Zaire!

A fuller account of these talks was given in a paper[23] I wrote for a British publication. My main conclusion on the issue of sanctions and outsiders interested in supporting 'The Struggle' was:-

"In complex situations a multi-pronged approach by outsiders, who are anxious to assist the resolution of conflict, may be more effective than a single mono-lithic approach".

No doubt some, mainly white, Zimbabweans will feel they were justified in resisting for as long as possible a take-over of their country by the Patriotic Front in 1980. It is impossible to know whether the country would have developed more peacefully and less destructively in the late 1990's if earlier initiatives had succeeded.[24] Over the years from 1958-9, when I was studying at St. Peters Hall (now College) in Oxford, we had occasional contacts with the late Bernard Chidzero and called him and his Canadian wife our "10 year friends". In 1959 I helped him with an anti-Federation Conference in Oxford, in 1969 we called on them in Nairobi and in 1979 we walked out to their house in the Geneva suburbs while the Lancaster House Conference was going on in London. He felt it had little chance of pulling of a peaceful settlement because the different sides were too far apart. In practice he became Zimbabwe's Minister of Finance up to his retirement on health grounds. During his time the Zim dollar did decline in value but the major collapse came later.

Our arrival in Zambia was disrupted by a serious car accident when a lorry pulled out in front of Theresa and our daughter on a main road. They fortunately had seat belts and were not too seriously injured. But the car was a write off and it took months for the lorry owners insurance to pay up. For our 1977 Christmas holidays we went by train from Kapiri Mposhi to Dar-es-Salaam by the Chinese Tazara Railway which was built to allow Zambia to bypass South Africa with exports of copper. In fact many of Africa's debt crises can be blamed on The Struggle. It was heavily subsidised and has still not been paid for. The train in 1977 ran absolutely to time with 60 second stops at small sidings but with no visible signs of Chinese supervision. Sometimes a hundred or more local peasants were waiting to do their twice weekly 60 seconds of business at one of the windows or doors! The cost of what is in many ways a white elephant is one of the "sacrifices made in the African liberation struggles" mentioned by Thabo Mbeki during Zambia's Independence Celebrations on 24 October 2004.

Much Chinese and Eastern Block aid to African countries was symbolic and not well planned. Zambia had a range of tractors donated from several countries without spare parts or training to keep them working for more than a few months. In one small attempt to promote trade with Zambia I investigated the vegetable, fruit and flower market in Moscow. While in Uganda during the first 15 months of Idi Amin I took part in a Farmers Forum in the huge International Conference Centre. It was an almost exact copy of Mulungushi Hall, built in Lusaka with Eastern Block aid for an Organisation for African Unity Conference in the 1960's. President Obote ordered it, presumably with a Yugoslav subsidy or loan of some sort, for the 1975 OAU Conference in Kampala. It was just ready in time for Idi's big promotion conference of farmers soon after the 1971 coup and was used for the OAU meeting when he was chairman. A major indication that we were under the Eastern Block sphere of influence were the 3 days of national mourning every time a Russian President died while we were in Zambia. This happened several times and, while bars were open we were not allowed to play tennis and with a later mourning even squash!

The major Eastern Block contribution to 'The Struggle' was supposedly in military training and hardware. A long train full of tanks and armoured cars rolled into the Lusaka Central Station in the early 1980's. They were too late for the Rhodesian conflict and probably made no significant impact on the South African settlement. In fact I feel we were fully justified in resisting the idea that the armed struggle would be the major factor in liberation. Archbishop Tutu had won the Nobel Peace Prize in 1984 and Chief Albert Luthuli won it in 1960 but Nelson Mandela had to wait until 1993 when it was awarded jointly to him and Mr. de Klerk. Amnesty International "would not campaign for us on the ground that we pursued an armed struggle", Mr. Mandela suggests in "Long Walk to Freedom" (page 603).

Oliver Tambo, who has been mentioned earlier, played a key role in the 1980's contacts with the South African Government. Around 1987, according to Allister Sparks, he said that "the ANC would seize any opportunity to negotiate if Pretoria showed that it genuinely accepted the need to create a non-racial society". "It would also run as a multi-party democracy with a mixed economy and in which basic freedoms would be guaranteed".[25]

It is interesting that Sparks' book was published in 1990, soon after the release of Nelson from prison and well before the eventual 1994 election. Much could have gone wrong in the process. His book would seem to confirm that much had gone on before 1990. In fact there were countless initiatives in business, religious, academic, political and diplomatic circles that came together to produce the eventual settlement. In 2000 we visited the village of Mells, near Bath in England to try to confirm that a South African Government-ANC-business men's meeting had taken place in the late 1980's. We got confirmation that Mells Park House then belonged to Consolidated Goldfields of South Africa – but little else! There is no doubt that a key meeting took place at Mells and that the South African Government were under intense pressure from the business community. In my own case Anglo American funded my 1988 lecture tour and took me to visit their agricultural projects near Giyani on the edge of the Kruger National Park.

The question that some will ask, in view of the poor image of African countries in the Western media, is: was all the support for "The Struggle" worth the effort? No one can avoid being disappointed at what has followed in certain countries. However overall I feel positive about the long-term future of Africa. This will be expanded on in the final chapter of this book. As regards those that supported in some way the struggle for liberation from Apartheid, minority rule in Rhodesia or colonialism our motives were fairly mixed. Above all we were supporting people we felt had been unfairly treated by a privileged minority for too long. "Separate Development" in South Africa and "Partnership" in the Federation might have worked if those who were supposed to benefit had a full say in their planning. The time for paternalism was over after the 1939-45 war.

European residents of South Africa and Zimbabwe couldn't realistically claim that they could have hung on to their privileges for a 1000 years as Ian Smith is supposed to have claimed. There is plenty of evidence from Kenya and Zambia that there should be a long-term place for expatriate westerners in the future. There will also be some who prefer to leave as will many indigenous people. When we stayed at the Bulawayo Club in 2002 we heard of a recent meeting for those wanting to know about emigrating to New Zealand. We were told that many were black Zimbabweans. There are also plenty of signs that NEPAD – New Partnership for Africa's Development – will lead to an influx of expatriate workers from a wide range of countries. The future of Africa, as for the whole world is to allow freer movement of people, particularly those with capital or skills to create jobs.

In most struggles it seems inevitable that the propaganda of the victors becomes the history of the vanquished. This is more likely to happen when peace is achieved without a degree of mutual respect. Hopefully South Africa's eventual history of The Struggle will reflect the full extent of multi-racial support and serve to promote the Rainbow Nation concept that helped the 1990's transition from the Apartheid state to one where everyone could contribute and have a say.

NOTES

1. Long Walk to Freedom by Nelson Mandela, Macdonald Purnell. Randburg, 1994, page 105.
2. R. Watts, Memoirs of the Refugee "Pipeline" – The Serowe Route, 1960-61. Botswana Notes and Records, Vol. 29.
3.
4. When living in KwaZulu/Natal from 1996-99 we once called on Ismail and Fatima Meer in Durban and heard of Ismail's imprisonment with a Quaker, Mary Barr, during the campaigns against the pass systems. Ismail was a friend of Nelson Mandela at Wits in 1943-44. Fatima helped him with the writing of "Long Walk to Freedom".
5. John Gunther. Inside Africa, page 331, Hamish Hamilton, London, 1955. Much later in the 1970's Michael Scott came for a rural weekend on our farm in Wales.
6. Gone with the Twilight, A story of Sophiatown by Don Mattera. Ravan Press, Johannesburg, 1987. This book gives a gripping account of the work of the Anti-Removals Committee and the role played by Robert Resha and his arrest in 1956 under the charge of High Treason (p.128). In 1961 Robert stayed with us in Serowe when being flown into exile where he died before the end of the struggle.
7. Alan Paton, Journey Continued, Oxford University Press, Oxford, 1988, page 179.

8. Letter dated 13 October 1960 from Sam Kahn to the author.

9. Our main involvement in the Rhodesian events was through Guy and Molly Clutton-Brock who moved to Bechuanaland after Guy's release from prison in 1959. They stayed with us from 12-15 October and several times in 1960 along with Mary Benson of the Africa Bureau in London. Guy gave an account of his and 494 other members of the African National Congress of Southern Rhodesia arrest and imprisonment on 26 February 1959 at the Oxford Conference I was involved in with Bernard Chidzero. This was later published in "A New Deal in Central Africa". Edited by Colin Leys and Cranford Pratt. Heinemann, London. 1960. By an extraordinary coincidence Colin and I were close boyhood friends in Bournville, Birmingham up to 1939. We both followed careers in Africa but met by chance on a footpath in the hills above Windhoek, Namibia in 1990.

10. Noni Jabavu, The Ochre People. John Murray, London, 1963.

11. Go Into All the World. Edited by Herbert and Beatrice Kimball, Friends United Press, Richmond, Indiana, USA 2002, page 44.

12. According to Stan Moore's autobiography page 31 his wife, Margaret, typed the Constitution on a stencil for running off in Salisbury. In 1962 she became Secretary of the City Branch of The Zimbabwe African People's Union (ZAPU).

13. Guy and Molly Clutton-Brock, Longman, Zimbabwe. Harare. 1987, page 131.

14. Luise Whilte. The Assassination of Herbert Chitepo, Indiana University Press, USA, 2003.

15. United Church of Zambia.

16. ZIPRA = Zimbabwe People's Revolutionary Army.

17. ZAPU = Zimbabwe African People's Union.

18. In 2003-4 we and other Quakers started getting letters from prisoners in Kabwe that we believe may have resulted from copies of The Friend sent to Richard. Attempts to get his sentence revised failed.

19. Zambian Daily Mail, December 14 1978.

20. Published as an occasional paper by the SA. Institute of International Affairs, November ;1980, Johannesburg.

21. H.W. van der Merwe, Peacemaking in South Africa – A life in Conflict Resolution. Tafelburg, Cape Town, 2000.

22. One talk on Zambia was given as part of a Symposium in Jan Smuts Hall covering Mozambique, Malawi and Zimbabwe, the latter talk being given by Eddie Cross, who was active in the Movement for Multi Party Democracy in the 1990's.

23. Ronald Watts "Some lessons from the South African Peace Process" in Medicine, Conflict and Survival, Vol. 12, 35-44 (1996), London.

24. Earlier initiatives included the Victoria Falls Talks of August 1975 and the Geneva Conference of 1976 (when Chidzero was an adviser to the Patriotic Front) plus abortive attempts to split the Patriotic Front in Lusaka funded by Tiny Rowlands of LONRHO.
25. Allister Sparks "The Mind of South Africa: The Story of the Rise and Fall of Apartheid", Heinemann, London, 1990, page 367.

CHAPTER IX

Africa's Disasters

AS THE LAST continent in the world to take off Africa was bound to have special problems. The disasters of collapsing economies, droughts, famines and health problems like HIV, TB and Malaria could have been predicted. The situation was made much worse by the precipitate withdrawal of colonial governments in the 1960's. This has already been covered in an earlier chapter. It is worth pointing out that the fact that the Portuguese stayed for 15 years after Harold Macmillan's "Winds of Change" speech implies that Britain, France, Belgium and Spain could have had a longer period of preparing their colonies for independence. The disasters in Angola and Mozambique post 1975 were largely the result of the sudden change of government in Portugal and the Cold War.

The key factors in Africa's disasters are concerned with economic collapse and indiscipline at several levels. George Kinoti, a Kenyan, was a contemporary of ours at Makerere University, Uganda in the 1960's. In the 1980's he became Dean of Science in Nairobi University and in January 1982 was kidnapped by a mob and led outside to be denounced as "an exploiter of peasants and workers".[1] In a book he described his experience of visiting Uganda shortly afterwards. "Makerere University in Kampala, where I once had been a student and later a teacher had sadly decayed from being a world-class university to something unrecognizable. Poverty, decay of institutions and infrastructure .... The beautiful and prosperous Uganda known in the 1950's and 1960's was no more". It is a tribute to African resilience that since the 1980's so much has been restored.

Some of the charities that support the struggles of Third World countries are critical of the role of western businesses in African countries. They are accused of paying low wages and promoting the export of food crops. The implication is that all African countries should concentrate on growing food crops for local consumption. In reality the countries that have succeeded in feeding their people without external aid are also the largest exporters of air freight vegetables, fruits and flowers. Both Kenya and Zimbabwe, before the late 1990's collapse caused by the farm invasions, kept their economies reasonably buoyant. Both had expanding air freight exports of vegetables and yet managed to keep their people supplied with food. Growing food crops and cutting down on exports is no guarantee that people in remote areas will get adequate food supplies in a drought. In fact in today's world no country can survive without earning foreign exchange through exports or tourism.

Africa's disasters can't be pinned down to one or even to a small range of causes. Even economic collapse can have many causes including corruption, failure to maintain tax revenues, diversion to, often unnecessary, military expenditure, discouragement of investors and luxury purchases for government elites. Tony Blair's Global Commission on Africa will only work if it recognises that a long hard slog is involved in avoiding future disasters. An African Union peace keeping force may help to reduce the number of genocide incidents. But there must be a major commitment to long-term measures such as Norway's 10 year agreement to support soil surveys in Zambia. Gradually western countries must massively increase their financial support for health services and education to correct the declines of the past 30 years. No country, even in the west, could cope with a doubling of population every 20 years. Yet American government aid and many aid agencies fail to recognize this basic fact that has undermined progress. Rapid...... population growth impedes progress not because of a shortage of land but because of a lack of the means to expand agriculture. Shortage of land is only a major cause of economic collapse in a few countries such as Rwanda and Burundi.

One of independent Africa's major disasters, as seen by western observers, is its tendency to develop dictators. The African Union has now resolved that it will not recognise changes of government by military coup. Yet Robert Mugabe was elected and

138

re-elected in several elections since 1980 and in many countries is considered to be a dictator. Over the past 50 years we have lived under what were in effect dictatorships in Zambia, Zimbabwe, Kenya and Uganda. However in these 4 countries only Idi Amin seized power by using the military. We lived next to Malawi in Eastern Zambia when Hastings Banda, in effect a dictator from 1966-1995, was removed in an election. In all these countries there were considerable numbers of opponents imprisoned. In retrospect leaders such as Kaunda, Nyerere and Moi were seen, after they lost power, as relatively benign compared with Robert Mugabe.

Our main close involvement in the fall-out of dictatorships was with a political prisoner in Lusaka Central Prison in the early 1980's. Theresa visited the prison as part of her medical research. A senior Malawi Army Officer heard she was a Quaker and said he had some contact with Lyle Tatum, an American Quaker representative in Salisbury, Rhodesia. He asked for our help because he said he had escaped Malawi without papers. He had been warned of a plot by the Head of the Army to eliminate him. We queued for a couple of hours to visit him in prison and pressed the UN High Commission for Refugees to get his release. During a party we introduced him to someone who was driving to Harare and he begged a lift. At the Chirundu border post he remained in the car and was able to cross without papers. On the strength of proving his mother was born in Rhodesia he claimed Zimbabwean citizenship and when last heard of had got an excellent managerial post. A legacy of the Central African Federation was that many Africans had multiple possibilities for claiming citizenship.

Our Malawian army officer was an extremely clever and resourceful man. We corroborated his story later on a visit to Britain when we phoned one of his Camberley senior military instructors. He remembered him well as one of their brightest officers but added that if we saw him again we should remind him of the £50 he had lent him which needed repaying! He is an example of the misuse of resources on the military after independence. Malawi, with no significant involvement in the liberation of Zimbabwe and South Africa, had no need of a large army. After independence on September 30 1966 Botswana decided not to have an army and depend on border police like Costa Rica. Much of the movement towards large standing armies was stimulated by Western governments. As long as an African dictator was considered to be on the Western side in the Cold War he was assured of subsidised arms supplies. When, in the late 1990's, a Quaker, Nosizwe Routledge, was appointed an Assistant Minister of Defence, there were hopes that the South African Government would reduce its expenditure on the military.

Civil wars, inter-tribal struggles and wars between countries have been extremely destructive during the 1970's, 80's, 90's and into the 2000's. I have no up to date figures of deaths in wars but the following for up to 1987 are enough to make the point:-

Numbers of deaths in selected Sub-Saharan African conflicts between 1895-1987[2]

COUNTRY	CONFLICT	YEARS	CIVILIAN DEATHS	MILITARY DEATHS
Angola	Independence	1961-75	30,000	25,000
	Cuba, SA & USSR & civil war	1975-87	200,000	13,000
Burundi	Hutu v. Govt.	1972-75	80,000	20,000
Ethiopia	Italy v. Ethiopia	1935-36	—	20,000
	Eritrean revolt & famine	1974-87	500,000	46,000
Kenya	UK v. Kenyan tribes	1895-96	1,000	—
	Mau Mau	1952-63	3,000	12,000
Namibia	German suppression of revolts	1903-08	80,000	—
Nigeria	Biafran War	1967-70	1,000,000	1,000,000
Rwanda	Tutsi v. Govt.	1956-65	102,000	3,000
South Africa	Boer War	1899-02	13,000	22,000
Estimated totals for all African countries from 1700-1987			46,992,000	47,922,000

It is difficult to draw detailed conclusions from this table but it is amazing that military deaths almost balanced civilian deaths. Presumably a very high proportion of civilian deaths were at the hands of the military and were the result of crossfire. The table provides valuable evidence for the campaign to restrict the sale of guns to African countries.

This table is an under estimate of the losses due to conflict and leaves out some major areas such as the Democratic Republic of the Congo (DRC). I was sent there in 1975 by OXFAM in a 2-man team when it was known as Zaire. We saw some of the havoc wreaked on the country's infrastructure in mindless conflicts. Almost every bridge had been destroyed in the area we visited. The

Agricultural Research Station had been looted and the library and records burnt. Fortunately some duplicate records were later tracked down to a government office in Brussels. I had visited the Belgian Congo twice in 1958, only 2 years before Independence. My impression was that much had been done to train people at intermediate levels. But all management positions were still firmly in the hands of Belgians. That was not a good omen for the approaching independence and the falling apart could easily be anticipated.

When in 1996 we moved to Mtunzini in KwaZulu/Natal we were quite soon aware of the gun violence that has affected many parts of South Africa for years. Theresa was employed at Ngwelezane Hospital and put in charge of the TB wards and out-clinics. Every Tuesday she was required to drive a government car to visit a range of clinics in the neighbouring hills. A Scottish surgeon was hi-jacked and killed soon after our arrival and a large number of hospital vehicles were stolen by gangs. Eventually I was given permission to drive government cars so that, with Theresa's Zulu assistant, we felt a bit safer. When I gave a talk to the Mtunzini Women's Institute I was surprised to hear an announcement that members should report for gun training. We found Mtunzini to be a relatively peaceful place and had no fence to our garden through-out our 4 years. As Quakers we considered these trends disturbing and we still carry on our South African Fiat a "Gun-free South Africa" sticker. There is a huge challenge for Africa to reduce the number of weapons and demilitarise the continent.

The chapter on the media was almost exclusively concerned with its impact on Africa. However from a western or even a world perspective Africa is seen as a continent of disasters – largely thanks to the all pervasive television media. This is not to say that there haven't been disasters or that the media have manufactured them. With such a large continent and so many countries there is at any one time always a famine, war or major health problem ready to be filmed. In 2004 Darfur provided an excellent opportunity for fill-ing TV news programmes when there was little news in the summer. It is worrying that much of the disaster image of Africa is driven by charitable bodies or organisations like the World Food Programme or UNICEF that are trying to pressure governments to act – and pay up! As I am writing this on November 7th 2004 a

BBC Radio 4 World Report Programme has just focused on the issue of disaster coverage. It was clear that the recent 20 year anniversary coverage of the Ethiopian 1984 famine on British media was not welcome in Ethiopia. The country now has an elected government and is striving to overcome its failed state image. Those involved in tourism revealed that the television programme had led to foreigners considering cancelling their bookings. Bob Geldof, who was involved in fund raising in 1984, is in 2004 a member of the Global Commission on Africa and determined to take a longer term view of Africa's problems.

Individual farmers can take years to fully recover from a major drought. Seeds of locally grown varieties of crops are used up and displaced by imported and often inferior types. The momentum of their farming calendar – cultivation of the soil, planting of seed, weeding and harvest – is lost. Nationally there is often a huge problem of regulating reserves to cover future shortages. Seasonal price variations, which should act as incentives to produce and store for seed during a shortfall, are disrupted. In short the effect of one famine can disrupt food production, storage and marketing for years. As I write in late 2004 famine is still very much on the media agenda with a continuing emergency in Darfur, Sudan and a new one in Eastern Kenya.

Our main experience of drought was in Zambia. From 1982-86 I was Research Extension Liaison Officer at the Central Research Station. This involved a lot of work to back up the plant breeders and agronomists with advice on varieties of crops and how to grow them. One clever initiative was to use a new irrigated farm on the shore of Lake Kariba to grow an out of season winter irrigated crop of a drought resistant sorghum variety to provide seed for the next summer season. This helped in a modest way to tide over the huge problem, after a drought, of lack of seed in the following year. We were promoting sorghum and millet as more drought tolerant crops than maize. I organised radio, press and television programmes to cover these approaches.

Another problem of drought is that of repaying credit for the crops that have failed. It is often impossible for the farmer to repay his previous credit and so qualify to get next year's credit for seed. This was a major concern of Professor Dumont[3] who we met in Lusaka when I was teaching at an agricultural college in 1979. He spoke to students and later met a few informally at our house in between his meetings with President Kaunda to discuss Zambia's agricultural problems.

Professor Dumont's advice to Kaunda was very similar to that being discussed by Tony Blair's Global Commission on Africa. How can aid which is labeled for the poor be more effective? How can the leakage of funds through corruption and inefficiency be reduced? How can credit for farm inputs be provided so that the whole system of marketing through co-operatives is not undermined? What can be done to make farming in Africa less dependent on erratic rainfall through small-scale irrigation? I had come across Dumont's book in the 1960's when teaching in East Africa. A brilliant review[4] by one of Kenya's early high flying civil servants had given me an African view of what he was saying.

Today's Kenyan politicians are regularly accused of incompetence and a host of other defects which are echoed in Dumont's book. Ndegwa lists them as follows:-

"corruption, alcoholism, ostentation, tribalism, lack of application and misapplication of known technology" plus "revolutionary speechifying".

The "essential reason" Dumont states in his book is a "frightening tendency to persist in 'errors of colonialism'". Having known Jeremiah Nyagah, a leading government minister, for several years and followed his career up to the end of the century I couldn't fault him on any of these counts. Kenya was fortunate to have at independence a number of dedicated and highly intelligent politicians. The corruption that crept in during the 24 year reign of President Arap Moi was largely among a few of the newer and younger politicians.

A major problem for action on food production is a lack of respect for tropical agriculture as a profession. For many years policy in Africa has been driven by aid organisations and charity administrators rather than by agriculturalists. The latest example is the campaign against GM varieties of crops where the last people to be consulted are plant breeders. African countries such as Zambia have been persuaded to refuse food aid if it includes GM crops. A leading critic of agricultural policies since the 1960's has been Basil Davidson who, as a historian, did a great job of correcting the impression in the west that African countries had no history to be proud of. However he went on to give the impression that virtually all actions of colonial governments were for the sole benefit of the ruling power. His views on export crops have become widely accepted in Africa and Europe. People in Britain still tend to boycott African goods such as vegetables or fruit because they say Africans should be growing food for themselves. He propounded the false theory that "the more that farmers turned to export crops, the less food could they grow for local use".[5] In practice the countries that maintained their exports, such as Ghana, have been those that have fed themselves best. In 2004 no country can avoid the need to export to pay for imports.

Although there was a great increase in corruption towards the end of Moi's reign the country remained reasonably stable except during elections. It is a mistake to think that all Africa's dictatorships were one-man shows. The one-party state of Julius Nyerere was an attempt to unify the country and prevent tribalism from disrupting the political scene. President Museveni preferred the option of a no-party state which seems to have advantages where the tribal balance has such a destructive potential as in Uganda. President Kaunda fell at the first multi-party election in 1990 but was replaced by a more corrupt government than his own. His "One Zambia – One Nation" slogan and his singing of "Tiyende Pamodzi" at rallies was a great effort to unify the country. Zambia's economy never really recovered from the economic crisis of 1975 when escalating oil prices coincided with a drastic fall in the world price of copper – the country's major export. Borrowing his way out of trouble contributed to the later debt problems. While there is a strong case for wiping out Third World debts it is essential that the same pattern is not repeated.

A table of currency values for Africa reveals in rough terms how well or badly they have managed their economies:-

AFRICAN COUNTRIES CURRENCY VALUES.
OCTOBER 2004

Country	US$	£	Euro
Gambia (Dalasi)	29.25	53.27	36.05
Ghana (Cedi)	9025	16435	11124
Kenya (Shilling)	81.30	148.1	100.2

144

Malawi (Kwacha)	108.8	198.2	134.2
Nigeria (Naira)	133.0	242.2	163.9
South Africa (Rand)	6.578	11.98	8.107
Tanzania (Shilling)	1079	1966	1330
Zambia (Kwacha)	4756	8661	5862
Zimbabwe (Dollar)	5605	10207	6908
Others (CFA Franc★)	443.4	807.5	546.6

★Applicable in Benin, Burkina Faso, Cameroon, CAR, Chad, Congo, Côte d'Ivoire, Gabon, Mali, Niger, Senegal and Togo.

When we went to work in Kenya in 1962 the currency was the East African shilling. It was in use throughout Kenya, Uganda and Tanganyika. With the break-up of the East African Community in the 1970's each country had a separate currency and exchange rates started to deviate. In October 2004 a British pound bought 148.1 Kenya shillings whereas it bought 1966 Tanzanian Shillings. This implies that Kenya has been better at managing its economy. Uganda revalued its shilling so a comparison is more difficult to make.

In the case of Zambia the Kwacha was launched in January 1968 with an exchange rate of 1 K = 10 Shs (£0.50). In other words a pound bought 2 Kwacha in 1968 and in October 2004 bought 8661 Kwacha. Zambian businessman, Murray Sanderson, wrote in 1994:[6] "Zambia's highest value note (was then) worth less than an American dollar". The Zimbabwe dollar was still worth something when we lived in Harare from 1990-93. I continued writing "Lighter Look" articles for the government paper *The Herald* after we left and paid my cheques into a Beverley Building Society savings account. I took my passbook on a recent visit to get it updated but with a balance of Z201.10 decided it wasn't worth the queueing. Fortunately I had withdrawn Z1800 in 1997. Among other crucial effects devaluation has drastically affected those living on pensions. The Zambian Fund we contributed to for Lazaro Banda in the 1970's gave him a pension that was not worth collecting.

Zimbabwe's currency problems have been accentuated by unrealistic exchange rates which allowed a two-tiered system to develop. A World Bank friend was asked by a bank clerk in Fort Portal, Uganda in the 1970's: "Do you really want me to cash that travellers cheque? I will only give you a tenth of what the man

145

standing outside the door will give you!" Also in the 1970's I had lunch in Kampala with the Manager of the Cadbury's chocolate factory in Nairobi. He had spent the morning buying the Ugandan cocoa crop. I asked him how much cocoa imported from West Africa or Malaysia cost when landed in Kenya. His reply implied that no one in his meeting had such a figure in mind. They had been plucking prices out of the air. Hopefully with more educated bank and government staff available such incidents have become less common. Hurried independence must have led to many such situations of topsy-turvey economics.

NGO's campaigning on Third World issues are fond of heaping the blame on the lenders for Africa's economic woes. The World Development Movement in 2004 published a report[7] with the subtitle: "How the IMF and World Bank have undermined development". It is encouraging that both authors are Zambian economists and policy analysts. This would not have happened in the early days of independence when the country had only 100 graduates. The report indicates that "Zambia had received only 5% of the debt reduction committed to it under HIPC".[8] But even if it receives full reduction "Zambia's debt service will continue to rise". They go on to accuse the IMF and World Bank of using the debt crisis "as another lever .... To wield influence over Zambia's economy" on issues like "privatisation and cuts in public spending". However there are a few bright spots such as the recent increases in world copper prices and the fact that Zambia had a maize surplus for export in 2003. It is interesting that Zambia's economy is benefiting from the exodus of white farmers from Zimbabwe.

I would hesitate to put all the blame for Africa's economic problems on the international bodies. Africa can only get out of the rut it has been in since the 1970's if there are policy changes in each country. Our main direct experience of ESAP – economic structural adjustment policies – was in Zimbabwe. We had known Bernard Chidzero since my year at Oxford in 1958-59. He became the Minister of Finance after independence and contributed a great deal to the stability in the 1980's. He was our MP in Avondale and we went to an election meeting in Prince Edward School where I had been teaching. ESAP, or what was then nicknamed "Ever Struggling African People"[9] had recently been launched. Our very reliable milk delivery man had just told us that he had been warned

146

that his company would stop delivering milk as its response to ESAP. I asked Bernard at question time whether this was the government's intention. He seemed shocked, said it was not their intention and our milk delivery continued. I have no idea whether this was the result of my question! It would have been better if I had raised the issue of fertilizer subsidies. In many countries there were drastic drops in fertilizer use when ESAP resulted in prices doubling or trebling. Many African soils are acutely deficient in phosphate and a failure to apply fertilizer led to drastic falls in yields or complete crop failures.

One of Africa's least accepted disasters is that of population growth. It was in Zimbabwe that I had an encounter over population issues with Dr. Richard Jolly of UNICEF. We had known each other at Makerere University and I had challenged him by supporting Dr. Maurice King's campaign to expose UNICEF's concentration on immunisation. UNICEF publicity included posters which claimed that a one dollar donation would save the life of a child. Our concern was to make sure that every child saved should be wanted and assured of care and education. I had written on these issues in the American journal *Rural Africana* in the 1960's and in the media chapter of this book there is an account of the TV programme in Zambia – "Does a farmer in 1984 need a large family?" In Zimbabwe I met Dr. Jolly at a reception when involved with UNICEF in producing textbooks on HIV/AIDS. He greeted me warmly but said jokingly that I was No. 2 enemy of UNICEF after Maurice. The problem is that his assurance that UNICEF's emphasis since the 1980's on "the importance of family planning and birth spacing" will take years to have an effect while immunisation had an immediate effect. One point made by Jolly, which I have never seen investigated, is that the tendency of the medical profession to keep control of family planning services and information on HIV/AIDS has slowed progress in these areas.

Another involvement with the population disasters in Africa is recent but has connections with school days. Dr. William Stanton, author of a definitive book on population growth,[10] was from 1940-48 a fellow pupil at Sidcot School, a Quaker school in Somerset. It is situated in the heart of the Mendip Hills which are built on limestone. From the age of 11 we enjoyed caving together. Sam, as he was known, took up Geology, but we both ended up in Africa.

In 1958, on my round Africa tour, he met me off the Leopoldville-Matadi railway and took me to the Maquela da Zomba copper mine where he was working as a geologist. After retiring to the UK he has become a leading authority on population.

In 1958 Angola was a typical Portuguese colony. On a second visit in 1973 the only hint I had of the coming independence it won in 1975 was that the Portuguese conscript soldiers we met seemed very unhappy. In 1975 I spent many breakfasts talking to an Egyptian Angola Conference delegate when I was stranded in the Kampala International Hotel. He implied there was a little chance of a peaceful resolution. In practice the 3 liberation movements, MPLA, UNITA and FNLA, continued fighting until the end of the Cold War. Stanton's book documents the effect on the people – "Up to a million refugees fled to the Congo" as a result of a pre 1975 revolt, and around 50,000 died. Stanton puts the total deaths during the civil war as about 1 million. During our time in Zambia (1977-86) I was a member of the Christian Council Refugee Committee which had responsibilities in the Angolan refugee settlement at Maheba to the north of the Copperbelt.

One of the anti-family size reduction arguments used in African countries has always been that in most countries there is plenty of land. For Zambia there is some truth in this as Stanton gives a population density figure of 13 people per sq. km. This compares with 285 for Rwanda and 212 for Burundi. Other low population densities include Gabon: 5, Botswana: 2.8, Zimbabwe: 32 and Kenya: 53. To put these figures in context Stanton has Wales at 143 and England at 382. On a recent visit to Kenya we picked up the following figures for provinces and districts[11]:-

Kenya – Selected rural population densities per sq. km. Provinces: Rift Valley: 138, Western: 406, Coast: 30. Districts: Vihiga: 886, Kisii: 758, Kiambu: 562, Machakos: 144.

An interesting fact for us is that Vihiga District is where nearly half the Quakers in the world are based. We lived there at the Kaimosi Mission from 1962-65. Our adopted daughter, Kageha Marshall was born there and has made two visits to her biological father who lives in nearby Nandi District. Another fostered child, Jennifer, died after we returned her to the family. Babies who lose their mothers when they are still suckling rarely survived in those days under village conditions.

Machakos District became the subject of a hot debate when an important book was published with the title: "More People, Less Erosion".[12] It is densely populated for an area subject to extreme droughts as at present (2004) and was treated to very critical comments by colonial agriculturalists such as Colin Maher. Their land was described as "a parching desert of rocks, sand and stone" due to over population of people and cattle. The colonialists did in fact teach terracing but this only took off after independence. Much of the recent prosperity is due to access to the Nairobi markets and many residents now commute daily to urban jobs. The title provides a gross distortion of the results of the research. On the other hand it provides an inspiring example of what can be achieved with good practices of compost use, terracing, moisture conservation and limited irrigation. It certainly does not provide any justification for increasing the population.

In fact what has done most harm in Africa is the rate of population increase. This is what is behind the failure to provide better education, health facilities, roads and job opportunities. In a fully developed economy a doubling of population in 20 years makes even keeping up with social needs through taxation impossible. But a major factor is the massive increase in government revenue through taxation that would be needed. This is a major issue in the debt crisis which will only partly be relieved by debt relief.

My second trip to Angola in 1973 was as a consultant on an interesting assignment for the International Coffee Organisation. Because of highly depressed coffee prices they started a Diversification Fund. The aim was to make coffee producing countries less dependent on the crop and reduce world supplies. For all the complaints about unfair trade one cannot escape the fact that low prices invariably result when supply exceeds demand. My role was to plan training initiatives to increase livestock production in Angola. I was never entirely happy in the role of consultant. When we were based in Wales for periods in the 70's and 80's our agreement was to limit any such trips to 2 months a year. The income from an international consultancy was enough in our case for a year since Theresa had a job. According to a recent article[13] the Department of International Development "spent £697 million on consultants to advise it about how to help the poor rather than actually helping the poor" ..... "in the past 5 years consultants have been paid more than £3 billion by the DFID". It is important that the entire philosophy of directing aid to the poor be questioned. When we visit African countries these days the biggest need is invariably "jobs". Handouts too often end up in the wrong hands.

The HIV/AIDS Disaster, which is now widely known and publicized throughout the world, was one that we experienced soon after it started in 1982. Theresa was then Professor of Community Medicine at the University Teaching Hospital in Zambia. She asked me if I would like to see a video in the medical school lecture hall about a new infection. It had been sent by the Centre for Disease Control in Atlanta, Georgia, USA. I attended and my main memory was that students were upset by an implication that it had originated in Africa. Another complication which affected their response was the fact that nearly all the early cases in the USA were among homosexual males. The essential need to inform people of how HIV/AIDS is spread has been complicated by a host of other factors. The policy in Southern Africa of migratory labour in mines with only housing for men has been a major cause of the spread of HIV.

The main positive response in the 1980's to the potential crisis in Zambia was the formation of Anti-AIDS Clubs in schools. This was initiated by Dr K. Baker, in the 70's one of Theresa's students, now living in Yeovil, England. These clubs taught about the syndrome and encouraged boys and girls to sign an agreement to remain chaste until marriage and faithful to one partner afterwards. If it could have had the necessary government and church backing and spread throughout Africa millions of lives would have been saved by now. When I returned to Zambia in 1987 I was asked by nuns near Lake Kariba what they could advise women in their congregation on how to protect themselves when their husbands returned from Lusaka. I said "condoms" but realised that it would be difficult advice for them to pass on. At lunch in Lusaka with the editor of the *Times of Zambia* I was told that AIDS was a subject they had to avoid. However President Kaunda did make a huge impact when he announced one of his sons had died of AIDS and said we should stop worrying about where it had come from and concentrate on where it is going. In 2004 the stigma of AIDS is still alive and prevents open discussion.

Theresa's main involvement with HIV/AIDS was when, in St. Francis Hospital, Katete (1993-95) Zambia and Ngwelezane

Hospital, South Africa (1996-9) she was in charge of tuberculosis patients. At least two thirds of TB cases in Africa also involve HIV/AIDS. What is not widely known is that the TB can be controlled with relatively cheap and simple drugs. For sometime she has felt that the campaign to make anti-retroviral drugs available in Africa was misplaced when so many TB cases were not getting the curative drugs and back-up. To be effective patients need to be supervised for several months, although they can go home for much of the period. Anti-retrovirals need even more intense instruction and follow up and, unlike TB, do not provide a cure. Both treatments have huge problems of drug resistance if not used properly. There is also confusion over how infective a PWA on anti-retroviral treatment is.

My involvement in HIV/AIDS was mainly as a journalist or teacher. In Zambia I joined a team at Katete that went to secondary schools. My role usually involved technical questions such as: "Can we get AIDS from a tooth brush or a mosquito bite?" The most effective person in the team was invariably the PWA (Person with AIDS). Teaching about condoms was always a problem because many churches opposed them. In Nairobi there was, for a time, an annual burning ceremony of donated condoms supervised by a Catholic Bishop and a Muslim leader. Such policies, encouraged by President Bush's and other US embargoes on family planning devices have resulted in thousands more HIV infections. On a November 2004 visit to The Gambia it was encouraging to see a US Peace Corps stand promoting condoms in an HIV/AIDS event held in St. Therese Church, Kanifing. Speaking on the eve of World Aids Day, President Jammeh said "young women and girls are more susceptible to HIV infections than men or boys". Regrettably female condoms did not seem to be widely available.

The reasons why the HIV/AIDS Crisis has escalated in Africa are many and some have been mentioned. A basic feature is that anything to do with sex is very difficult for parents to discuss with their children in most societies. A women's group I spoke to near Empangeni in KwaZulu/Natal told me they couldn't speak to their daughters about these issues. In Zimbabwe I was part of a team drafting secondary school textbooks on HIV/AIDS. I was rather bizarrely assigned some culture chapters and found out that in Shona (and many other) cultures such instruction is done by aunts or grandmothers. A major problem is understanding what a "syndrome" is. Also that an action one evening, perhaps under the influence of alcohol or drugs, can lead to infection that will only show in 2, 3 or 4 years. In Kenya and South Africa I made attempts to talk in schools on AIDS but got very few responses. In Zimbabwe an article I wrote in the Quaker weekly *The Friend* produced an immediate phone call and the despatch of 10 copies of a medical text book on AIDS. Several schoolboys told me it was only the stark pictures in this book that convinced them that AIDS was real.

Health assistance cannot be broken down to subsidising one or a set of drugs as in the case of anti-retrovirals. Other sexual infections increase the risk of HIV transfer enormously. The West must start to think of across the board help with health services in Africa. The emphasis needs to be more on prevention, education, family planning, HIV testing and child health. In a sense President Mbeki was right when he said AIDS is a disease of poverty. He could have added "a lack of education". The confusion in Zimbabwe where I found primary school children asking about getting AIDS from sharing toothbrushes was alarming. I discovered a teacher's guide issued in the 1980's which had "sharing a toothbrush" and "many sexual partners" next to each other in a diagram on AIDS infection routes.

Failures to develop industries and fully developed marketing are in part due to colonial policies. Travelling from West to East across Africa in 1958 it was noticeable that countries such as Uganda, Kenya and Rhodesia did not have large open markets as in Nigeria. Imports and marketing of produce were often handled by the Asian or European communities. It was more difficult for Africans to break into marketing and manufacturing. A very detailed report which aimed at more "African Socialism" looked into these issues in 1968.[14]

Doubtless we will see more disasters in the coming years. The most that can be hoped for is that Western responses will be timely, appropriate and long-term. Much of the famine response has been too short-term. Providing food for the starving is only a small part of the solution. Much more follow-up is needed to prevent recurrence of disasters. Several years are needed with a focus on increased irrigation plus ensuring seed and fertilizer supplies. While I have always been enthusiastic about organic solutions, such as compost, they cannot solve Africa's many nutrient deficiencies particularly of phosphate. I have recently been trying to publicise the research by fellow Quaker agriculturalist, Vernon Gibberd, to develop small-scale rainwater catchments and a compost toilet system in South Africa.

Some future disasters are certain to involve outbreaks of disease and a few will be new diseases. There is already, as I write in 2004, concern about a goat that was infected with BSE[15] in France (*The Times* 2/11/04). This seems unlikely to develop like the BSE in cattle scare in the 1990's because there is now strict control over the feeding of animal material to animals. However a serious goat disease would have a direct effect on Africa which in 1966 had 40% of the world's population of goats (FAO Report). The main British groups that eat goat meat are Muslims and Afro-Caribbeans but in the Middle East consumption is huge. Western countries have tightened their import controls because of a range of diseases and impurities. An example is groundnuts which are a popular export from West Africa. According to Grain South Africa (*Farmers Weekly* 15/10/04) "The EU protects itself from imports with food-safety standards". Africa faces an uphill task in using agricultural exports to solve her economic problems but has few other options except for those countries with oil or mineral reserves.

NOTES

1. Hope for Africa by George Kinoti. International Bible Society, 1994, Nairobi, Introduction.
2. Figures extracted from Table in:-
   Sivard, R.L. World Military and Social Expenditures 1987-88. 12th Edition.
   World Priorities Inc. Box 25140, Washington, D.C.
3. René Dumont (1904-2001). False Start in Africa. André Deutsch London. 1966. Originally published in French.
4. Philip Ndegwa, Chief Planning Officer Ministry of Economic Planning and Development. Review in East Africa Journal. March 1967.
5. Basil Davidson. Modern Africa. Longman, London, 1983, page 19.
6. Times of Zambia. 7 December 1994.
7. Zambia: Condemned to debt by Situmbeko and Zulu. 88 pages. WDM 25 Beehive Place, London SW9 7 QR. April 2004.
8. HIPC = Heavily Indebted Poor Country debt relief.

9. Alternatives are: Extra Suffering And Poverty
   Even Sadza's A Problem
10. William Stanton. The Rapid Growth of Human Populations 1750-2000. Multi-Science Publishing Co. Ltd. 5 Wates Way, Brentwood, CM15 9TB, UK. 2003.
    (NB. The book covers at least 55 African countries with graphs and population statistics plus an historical summary.)
11. Institute of Economic Affairs. The Little Fact Book. 2002. Published by Friedrich Ebert Stiftung, P.O. Box 59947, Nairobi.
12. Mary Tiffen et al More People, Less Erosion. Environmental Recovery in Kenya, 1994. John Wiley & Sons Ltd. Chichester, UK.
13. *Daily Telegraph*. 11 October 2004.
14. National Christian Council of Kenya "Who Controls Industry in Kenya". Report of a Working Party. E.A. Publishing House, Nairobi, 1968.
15. BSE = Bovine Spongiform Encephalopathy.

CHAPTER X

Africa's Future

AT THE END of our 50 years of involvement in African countries there is some hope that Africa and its problems is coming nearer the top of the world's agenda. Probably the most hopeful period of the past 50 years was in the countries where we worked soon after their independence. Many countries had a period of stability when their economies were still reasonably strong, aid was flowing from a range of countries and armies were small or non-existent. We have lived through so many declining situations since that we can perhaps be excused for being cynical about some of the hype over what the EU or the G8 can achieve. Unrealistic slogans such as "Health for all by the year 2000" and "Make Poverty History"[1] will not inspire confidence unless some of the less popular issues are tackled. They concern questions such as rapid and unsustainable population growth, plus keeping checks on future debts which may be incurred for prestige projects. While trade issues are critical to Africans solving their own problems the subject is extremely complex. Freer trade could put African countries at the losing end of export drives by countries like China and India. But tariffs and subsidies should in future be reserved for the poorer countries and not used to flood world markets with products that undermine African farmers' prices. Western subsidies could be considered for fertilizer and seeds, the cost to be set against savings on famine relief. While there are demands for "reparations for the effects of the slave trade" a more effective approach would be on-going contributions towards education, agriculture and health.

Part of this final chapter was appropriately written in The Gambia. Appropriate because my second letter from Africa, written in August 1954 had the heading "Off Gambia". It took 50 years for me to set foot in this West African country. I still have vivid memories of Freetown, Sierra Leone, where we landed on the 8th August 1954. I paired up for the day with a student friend who I knew at Reading University. My letter home refers to "The Heart of the Matter" by Graham Greene and the film of the same title. The open drains in the town had made a deep impression on me. I wrote that "on the whole my first encounter with Africa has been very pleasant". At least I started on a hopeful note!

From the port in Freetown we were surprised to find a double decker bus service to town. My friend dropped his dark glasses on the floor and someone shouted that they had found them as we got off. I commented: "In view of the poverty most people live in such honesty was quite a surprise". My friend had been to India and thought "the poverty and slums were far worse in India". On our 2004 visit to The Gambia we saw incredible poverty but had the feeling that, even in the heart of the slum we were taken to, we were safe. The main need that people in Africa express more and more is for jobs. This is what they hope for rather than to be lifted out of poverty by handouts. The doubling of what governments raise in taxation with aid from the west would get away from the "hand-out philosophy" of much aid to Africa at present. Tackling poverty is a worthy aim for the Commission for Africa but involves much more analysis of why Africans are too poor and western countries are too rich. A slowing down of some western economies may be essential if we want other countries to catch up.

The Gambia, like every African country, needs to earn more foreign exchange and a major source at present comes from Western Europe. The tourist season is limited to the dry period from November to May. This may partially account for the incredible welcome given to people escaping the European winter in Britain, Holland, Germany and Scandinavia. The warmth of the Gambian spirit helps to make up for the lack of wild animals that many westerners expect. While we were there, John, the last indigenous lion, was shot dead when he escaped from a fenced area of Abuko Nature Reserve. We protested that nowadays it is possible to "shoot" with an anaesthetic dart before moving dangerous animals. The only hope for Africa's wildlife is that tourism will continue and hopefully involve a wider range of countries.

One day we witnessed a remarkable 50 year reunion between two old Gambian colonials – Henry Oliver, Commissioner in Basse at the furthest section of the Gambia River, and his Agricultural Officer, Ralph Liney. Henry stayed on after independence in business for many years while Ralph moved to Sierra Leone and then back to Britain with his wife, Jean. When they were in Gambia the population was about a quarter of what it is in 2004 (Approx. 1.5 m). Our talk with them came shortly after a hot discussion with a Swedish professor when he lumped slavery and colonialism together as the twin evils inflicted on Africa. I pointed out that, once established, colonial rule in Africa, as Roman rule in Britain, created some order and progress. I find it hopeful that historians like Niall Ferguson[2] are starting to correct the totally negative image of colonialism created by Basil Davidson et al. If Africa can follow Britain's example of forgiving the Romans it should be easier for both to work together in future. It will take time but I am hopeful it will happen over the next fifty or one hundred years. It deserves to be repeated that a key to Africa's recovery is a rebuilding of trust and respect.

The Gambia received independence on February 18 1965 when the Duke of Kent presided at the event. The last Governor, Sir Paul Foot, who became Governor-General after independence was apparently bored with the job. In a recent obituary he is quoted as saying: "It seemed the only way out was to write a republican constitution. I did so. We put it to the electorate, and they rejected it".[3] A republic was later declared on April 24 1970 after a second referendum.

One of the things that has helped to raise our hopes for Africa is the way that Gambia has developed its tourism. At the time of independence there were only a few 100 per year.

By 1990 there were 55,000 and by 2000 there were well over 100,000. Being driven down to Gunjur, near the border with Senegal we saw some 5-star hotels under construction. This expansion has been developed in competition with destinations like The Maldives, Goa plus East and South Africa. Under Gambian direction local developers and builders have worked with companies from Western Europe. We have been impressed with the level of Gambian involvement and the friendly relations between tourists and local people, some of it built up over several repeat visits. The company we went with "The Gambian Experience" make a point of encouraging such friendship. They also encourage their hotels to buy local produce so as to generate more jobs.

The colonialists are still often blamed for Africa's troubles because of their creation of arbitrary borders following the Berlin Conference of 1884-5. The Gambia is a good example. According to one guide it was once described as a "geographical absurdity". How well can it survive into the twenty first century? In the 1970`s and 80`s. President Jawara, of Gambia was a personal friend of President Senghor of Senegal. Senghor helped Jawara to get back after a coup in 1981 but the confederation of the 2 countries only lasted from 1981 to 1989. Hopefully the proposal for a Sene-Gambian Federation will be revived when present opposition subsides.

In the post war era of 1945-65 there was much hope generated for a range of federations which would overcome some of the colonial border problems. I was active in opposing the Central African Federation because it was being imposed against the wishes of African leaders. In retrospect I regret this because it might have prevented the rise of dictatorships like those of Banda and Mugabe. Kamuzu Banda ruled what in effect was a one party state for 30 years but managed the economy much better than his neighbours Zambia and Tanzania. Both arose out of tribal rivalries for power. Renewed hope may be aroused by moves to revive the East African Community. Certainly Gambia would be better off in the long run if it was associated closely with neighbouring countries. Unless there is considerable mineral wealth or an oil discovery a country of 1½ million will find it difficult to attract investment. Tourism is only a partial answer for small countries like The Gambia and is very vulnerable to unforeseen events like the Indian Ocean tsunami of December 2004.

Kenya's even bigger tourism industry is regularly undermined by terrorism warnings put out by the U.S. Embassy. A major problem for The Gambia is that tourism is almost entirely confined to the European winter from October to April. My taxi driver for a tour of agricultural exporting companies complained he had no income from May to September.

An extraordinary colonial hangover, in some ways, Gambia seems to survive on its Englishness. The coastline is identical with

158

many neighbouring, former French colonies. Scandinavians and some Germans and Dutch could find a destination where most people speak English easier.

Of the 16 excursions offered by The Gambian Experience, our package company, we chose "Roots". It is designed to introduce visitors to the tragic history of the slaves that were exported in the seventeenth and eighteenth centuries. I spent part of the 5 hours on board the small Spanish passenger boat Joven Antonia reading a book on slavery which ended with a section on "Who's to Blame?" To quote: "At the beginning of the twenty-first century a number of South African, Caribbean and African states called for the UN to declare colonialism and slavery to be crimes against humanity" ... "They also demanded reparation or compensation for the long-term effects that slavery has had for the poverty and racial tensions that have blighted so many lives". Whether these claims, particularly in the case of colonialism, would stand up in a court of law, is highly debatable. A colleague at Makerere in the 1960`s and 70`s was Ali Al`Amin Mazrui (born Mombasa, 1933), who left to pursue a career in political science in the U.S.A. Despite coming from an Arab family that once traded slaves, he led a campaign in the United States to demand reparations for the harm done by the Atlantic Slave trade. What gives more cause for hope is that the prosperous countries will one day wake up to the fact that the division between rich and poor countries cannot go on widening for ever. Regular contributions to education, health and such things as roads would be more effective than any one off payment to compensate for slavery.

We enjoyed our small short-wave radio while in The Gambia and listened avidly to the BBC World and African news, which we find difficult to get in Wales. One item that struck home was Desmond Tutu's warning in the annual Nelson Mandela lecture in Johannesburg on the 23rd November 2004. He said South Africa is sitting on a "powder keg" because millions are living in "dehumanising poverty". He was critical of the Black Economic Empowerment Programme (BEE) which he said was enriching blacks who were already wealthy. The micro-credit programmes, which have been so successful in Asia, seem to provide the greatest hope for overcoming poverty.

The BEE policy is similar to the Africanisation or Indigenisation policies of newly independent African states. At the time they were quite understandable and justified. We both held jobs where we were `Africanised` and accepted that we had to move on. However when continued over a long period they stultify development and should be discontinued. If the rest of the world is to work with Africa to create jobs it must be allowed more access to jobs to get economics moving. The brain drain of African nurses and doctors to Europe cannot be entirely stopped. Hopefully more Westerners can be encouraged to fill some of the vacant positions in Africa.

In spite of Messrs. Blair and Brown's strong statements about Britain's future commitment to Africa there is widespread scepticism amongst the public about the effectiveness of aid. Rachel Sylvester had a prominent article shortly before we left for The Gambia headed: "Do all these consultants really benefit the Third World?"[4] Over 50 years I have had 3 consultancies with international organizations – IFAD, FAO and the International Coffee Organisation – lasting approximately 2-3 months each. According to Rachel "DFID spent £697 million on consultants to help the poor rather than on actually helping the poor" in 2003. The big question is how do you help the poor without creating massive dependency. The cry we hear in Africa every time we go is: "we want work"!

There is little chance of replacing consultants in the short term. They work best on projects that have clear economic objectives. However many have been diverted by the new emphasis on poverty orientation, grass roots initiatives and the "in-terms" for development work over 30 years – such as Adaptive Research and Participatory Development. In my short experience of consultancies directed at agriculture the key areas which are neglected are processing, marketing, prices, input supplies plus savings and credit – which cannot be separated as they so often are. Marketing cooperatives, which held out great hopes for farmers in the 60's and 70's, were wrecked by too easy credit and too little attention to recycling funds.

On our return from The Gambia in December 2004 I started to read 2 books which relate to Africa's future. One was the record of a conference in Nairobi designed to establish a partnership between the World Bank and "the faith communities".[5] The second[6] is the life story of an Anglican agricultural missionary, Stephen Carr, who worked for the World Bank from 1978 to 1989. Stephen started his service as a missionary to Nigeria in 1952 and retired to a Malawi small holding in 1989. At the age of 77 he is still active, with Christian Aid and USAID funding, in supporting small-scale farmers with seeds, techniques and inputs. His faith in the abilities of small-scale farmers to solve their problems and respond to fair prices for what they produce is undiminished. The latest programme he is promoting in Malawi is a U.S. funded scheme to pay farmers in fertilizer for extending rural road networks. The fact that the World Bank sought to recruit Stephen and to promote him so that from 1987-89 he was in charge of "All of Sub Saharan Africa's" agricultural projects was impressive. He appears to have turned round several projects so that farmers got better deals and fairer prices for crops. We visited Stephen's Nyakashaka and Wambabya settlement projects in Uganda during 1966-70 and still consider them to be models of how to develop new areas for farming at minimum cost. Both survived the disruptions during the Idi Amin period from 1971 to 1979. Hopefully "the faith communities" involved in the Nairobi Conference will find more agricultural missionaries. The future of Africa for areas where there are no minerals or oil, lies with farmers. The Malawi Government is to be congratulated for offering Stephen and his wife 'permanent residence' to retire in Malawi and hopefully other governments will follow their example.

Stephen Carr's 50 plus years of service to Africa has been remarkable and in the agricultural field almost unique. The idea that after independence African countries could get rid of expatriate staff and gradually employ only nationals has not worked. The increased flow of aid, which is so urgently needed, depends on having a corps of expatriates with long African experience. This applies to health, education, road construction, urban planning and a host of other spheres. Hopefully the Commission for Africa will give attention to such long-term needs. A major increase in Western aid to Africa cannot be managed without a determined effort to create such a corps. The idea of a partnership between Africa and western countries depends on having the right people on the ground.

161

Most African countries are failing to pay their workers adequate wages and almost no funds are available for travel, housing and the infrastructure to produce development. Road maintenance is totally inadequate and when, as frequently happens, a colonial bridge is washed away in a flood, there are no funds to build a new one. Independent governments have been unable to raise taxes to pay for all these essentials. The present project approach involving consultants needs to be supplemented by something like the old Development and Welfare grants to African budgets. To build trust between western and African governments budgeting aid could be on a rising scale depending on auditors' reports. Most African countries fall down badly on tax collection and aid on a percentage basis would encourage greater diligency. A number of countries have in recent years benefited from British personnel to back up revenue earning departments such as Income Tax and Customs. This assistance should be offered to a wider range of countries.

A major deception in the West, displayed in relation to Africa, is that economic growth will eventually allow Africa to "catch up". The idea that the whole world can follow the West in its pursuit of "economic growth" is in any case discredited. If we are serious about Africa "catching up", it will be essential to consider how the West can "slow down". In the 50 years we have been in and out of Africa there has been some economic progress in most of the countries we have worked in. But overall the trend in a whole range of areas has been downwards. They include:- availability of a good free education, a reasonable standard of housing, roads and transport, and a free and effective health service. The situation has reached the point where only long-term budgetry support will raise standards and hopefully slow the steady flow of trained health and other workers to western countries.

The Fair Trade Movement in western countries is an encouraging development. However it is difficult to see it going much further in its present form. Too much of the processing and packaging, particularly of cocoa, tea and coffee, is done in Europe. It is still difficult to go into a supermarket and buy African products. Many labels take the easy way out by stating: "Produce of more than one country". At one stroke it would be possible to favour several African countries if customers were persuaded to buy cane sugar only. Most of the white sugar we buy comes from sugar beet grown in Europe with enormous subsidies. Some people boycott African fresh fruit and vegetables because they are air freighted. While we need to reduce our use of oil it should be recognized that thousands of Africans depend on this trade for jobs. In the case of Gambia much of this fresh produce is transported on planes shared with tourists. Fair trade needs to incorporate the concept of adding value through processing and packaging in the African country where produce is grown.

Dr. George Kinoti, the Kenyan Professor mentioned earlier, ended the conference we attended in Kenya shortly before we moved our base from KwaZulu/Natal to Wales with these words:-

"Reasons for hope can be found in understanding the complex causes of poverty and in observing that poverty can be drastically reduced, as has occurred in China". Earlier he had said "the five poorest countries in the world are located" in East Africa.[7]

The mention of China was interesting because this conference was designed to promote development issues amongst Christians. In the book which was mentioned in an earlier chapter Dr. Kinoti emphasized rapid population growth as a key issue in tackling poverty. He stated (page 62) "Most Africans consider it a blessing". But he goes on rightly to state "the population is growing faster than the economy". China's success in tackling poverty was due to many factors – but reduced population growth has been crucial. Dr. William Stanton indicates a population growth rate drop from 2.2% per annum in 1960 to 1.4% in 2000. According to Dr. Kinoti (page 63): "The challenge is for Africans to take the initiative in slowing down population growth and at the same time promote food production and economic growth". The hopeful part of Dr. Kinoti`s book is that he urges "Africans to take the initiative in slowing down population growth".

The Republic of Cameroon is where I got slightly involved in population issues in 1989. I had gone there as part of a team of consultants working for IFAD. During briefing in Rome I was amazed at the opulence of the IFAD offices for an organisation that professed to be tackling Third World poverty. Our task was to conduct an Appraisal Mission into a proposal to supply major new funding for the MIDENO project in NW Province. The project was directed at increasing the output and income of small-scale farmers. I put in a supplement – an appendix to the report drawing attention to the absence of family planning facilities in the area. This was not in our "terms of reference" but I considered it important when the following were considered:-

Average farm family size = 7.2.
Average size of farm (ha) = 1.2 in Momo Division

Hopefully population issues will be tackled in all the new aid initiatives.

The Gambia is a good place to look at poverty, aid and what Britain has done and could do. Most of the post war projects failed on technical grounds such as ill judged soils, rainfall and over-mechanisation. On the strength of my agricultural journalism we were invited to visit the Central Agricultural Research Institute (CARI) near Banjul Airport. We were shown a line of PhD theses completed at Reading, Bangor and other institutions over 15 years. But their beautiful facilities were woefully under-utilised because of a lack of funding for basic expenses. Hopefully where the new aid initiatives find well staffed research programmes they will ensure adequate funding. A danger will be that all aid funding will be tied up in large, easily supervised, grandiose programmes.

The book I edited in 1969, "New Hope for Rural Africa", has been followed by other books with similar titles. One was "New Hope for Africa" by Merfyn Temple[8] which is an account of his journey with a bicycle from Nairobi to Kariba in 1989. Merfyn pins his hopes for Africa on organic farming. "The organic method of agriculture gradually improves soil fertility and is therefore indefinitely sustainable". One of the first places he visited was Manor House Agriculture Centre, near Kitale in W. Kenya. While Theresa was teaching in Moi University I was on the board at Manor House. Bio-intensive horticulture, which is what they taught, is similar to other organic systems as promoted by the Soil Association, which I then belonged to. I resigned when I found a neighbour in Wales "going organic" because it was more profitable. I felt "organic" production had taken off and no longer needed my support. In Africa I have problems with the idea that organic systems work everywhere. Manor House is in a high altitude area with good soils and rainfall. The majority of African farmers are on poor soils with very erratic rainfall. I have seen areas in Kenya where nothing will grow without phosphate fertilizer. However I hope that Merfyn's

164

advocacy of animal draught for ploughing – with donkeys or oxen – will succeed. Tractor farming in Africa will for sometime be restricted to largely commercial farms.

A major impression on returning to Wales was of the increasing materialism causing many problems in British society. The 2004 American presidential election reinforced this view of the United States, where we have many long standing friends from our years in Africa. Africa has failed in many western eyes because it has not developed economically. As Trevor Huddleston stated in the Foreword to "New Hope for Rural Africa":- "Our poverty is not the daunting, depressing, squalid poverty of the urban slum: it is the poverty of freedom and opportunity". The poorer countries in Africa such as Tanzania often inspire more hope than the richer.

One of the 'Hope' books mentioned earlier was published 50 years ago.[9] Dr. J.H. Oldham: "an acknowledged authority on African affairs" since 1925, wrote it to promote the Capricorn Africa Society. This was a brave attempt to head off the sort of black nationalism promoted eventually by Robert Mugabe. It was the unlikely brainchild of the founder of the SAS during the Second World War – Colonel David Stirling. He had moved to Southern Rhodesia in 1946. In 1956 a CAS conference in Salima, Nyasaland was attended by 250 Africans, Europeans and Asians. According to Oldham Herbert Chitepo helped him write the book. As described earlier Herbert was assassinated near Lusaka in 1975. Stirling's original idea was a Federation of 6 countries in East and Central Africa. His promotion of the concept of 'partnership' between black and white became ridiculed once it became clear that whenever they could white settlers would hold the reins. When we moved to Harare in 1990 we were told by settlers on an adjoining table in the Jameson Hotel: "You will find the natives here very friendly"!

In a study of the Capricorn Society Richard Hughes[10] stated: "We remained Sancho Panzas after the Don had left the field". The CAS failed to convince Africans that they could pull off a new deal under the Central African Federation – but there is much to be said for revamping the idea in the 21st century.

Basil Davidson, a British historian who started his African studies in 1951, has for years been a critic of colonial rule. In 1983 he wrote[11] (page 11). "Many hundreds of states and communities lost their independence to the various European colonial powers". "All were gathered into some 50 colonies marked out by frontiers that were new". Many observers predicted a falling out over borders between newly independent states. But as Davidson points out (page 253) one of the principles of the Organisation of African Unity Charter was "Respect for the existing frontiers of member states". There were also clauses covering "non-interference in internal affairs" and "peaceful settlement of all disputes". The expected flare up of violence over the imperial boundaries has not happened. Hopefully this situation will continue under the new African Union (AU) which replaced the OAU.

It is difficult to see how any other policy was possible at the time that so many countries were given their independence. The acute problem areas are borders with oil or mineral reserves such as the Bakassi Peninsula between Nigeria and Cameroon. While borders have been a problem in various countries since they gained independence it is difficult to see how these would have been avoided if there had been no colonisation. Hopefully in future full use will be made of the International Court of Justice.

What hope is there that the western media will play a more positive role in Africa in the coming years? In South Africa the western media was a crucial factor in the eventual overthrow of Apartheid. It was generally more sympathetic than in the case of the continuing Palestinian struggle, partly because the level of violence on the ANC side was much less.

As I write this on November 11th 2004 news is coming through of the death of Jasser Arafat and plans for a grand funeral in Cairo. So there was at last an African element to the Palestinian cause.

A current on-going issue is that of Darfur in Sudan. The BBC has given massive coverage to Fergal Keane's report on the evacuation of a refugee camp on the edge of Nyala. Fergal appeared to make little attempt to get an official explanation of what was going on. The government side was put in a short interview with the Sudanese Ambassador in London. I visited OXFAM in Nyala on my way to a Quaker project at El Geneina on the Chad border in 1988. I can confirm the government explanation that the UNHCR policy was to site their camps several kilometres from a neighbouring town. In this case they were having difficulties because of the closeness of the camp. A decision had been made to move to a

166

new site away from the town. A major problem had been to keep refugees separate from local people seeking famine relief food. Fergal seemed to make no effort to find out what was behind what was undoubtedly an inhumane action by the authorities. Repeated cries of 'genocide' and demands for UN action have done little to ease the situation. Dr Colin Morris's appeal on BBC Radio 4 (13/12/04) for "less militant righteousness" by the west could be applied to other situations in Africa.

The British journal *The Lancet* has in 2004 taken a much greater interest in economic policies. A doctor working with children in Kampala[12] in a lengthy article accuses his government of following an economic policy "which extols the export-oriented private-sector" ... "at the expense of social welfare". Both Uganda and Botswana are held up by western governments as economic successes. The doctor claims that Uganda's economic model "largely favours foreign investors and multi-national companies".

Dr. Okuonzi's thesis would carry more weight if he presented an alternative to the present dependence on aid, exports and foreign investment. Ivory Coast has fallen apart mainly because of the 5 million migrant workers from neighbouring countries who were allowed to settle but later had their citizenship taken away. The doctor is right to support improved social services but needs to find ways that will allow them to be paid for. If NEPAD is to work foreign investment will be needed and export earnings increased. A study needs to be made of the Chinese investment in Lesotho where a substantial export orientated textile business has been built up.

We have no regrets about our decisions to keep looking for posts in African countries where we could continue to serve the needs of African people. When we returned to our Welsh farm in 1999, after 10 years continuous residence in Zimbabwe, Zambia, Kenya and South Africa, we felt like aliens. So much had changed in terms of standards of living, technology, and the speed of change. After 5 years we are still trying to come to terms with what in many ways is a new society. In general our relative optimism about Africa is a result of our pessimism about the long-term sustainability of western countries. With all the disasters which have been covered most Africans live in a more sustainable way than most westerners. They could also be better placed to survive some major disasters.

Since returning to Wales we have made 2 visits to Zimbabwe, 3 to South Africa, 2 to Kenya and 1 each to Tanzania, Namibia and Gambia. Each time we are refreshed and enthused by the people we meet. In these visits to East and Southern Africa, – Zimbabwe, Namibia, Kenya, Lesotho, Botswana and South Africa we have seen renewed interest in irrigation as one answer to food security in drought-prone countries.

Small-scale projects, that can largely be operated with local labour, bring great hope for some communities. The Dabane Trust, operating from a base in Bulawayo, Zimbabwe does an excellent job in teaching villagers to collect water in sand rivers using small dams or weirs. Stephen Hussey, a British Quaker who started the Trust, has recently been awarded a PhD for his thesis on pumps that can extract through sand.

Vernon and Tineke Gibberd, who we visited in 2003 near Queenstown in South Africa, are showing how 2 people can grow most of their own food using flash flood water collected in underground tanks called Hafirs. The water is dripped onto vegetable plots using ordinary plastic pipe and fertility is increased with a compost toilet. (For details see South African Farmer's Weekly 16/4/04) But in countries that still have rapid population increases there may still be a role for larger dams. If well designed these should provide hydro-electricity, water for irrigation and fish. Davidson (Modern Africa p. 237) is critical of such schemes because of displacement of people, siltation, dangers of weed spread, parasitic diseases and "ecological degradation". Such criticism cannot be taken very seriously unless there is some promotion of family size limitation.

One of the hopeful developments in the world during the past 10 years has been the way that tobacco is now generally regarded. When we moved to Harare for Theresa to take a post of Senior Lecturer in Community Medicine we had no idea of how critical tobacco was to the Zimbabwe economy. In 1991 tobacco had contributed 36.5% of all Zimbabwe export earnings. I arrived with a negative feeling for "the weed", having retired from teaching in Zambia 10 years earlier partly because of my objection to several 5 hour staff meetings smothered in smoke. However one of the Lima Time TV programmes I did was sponsored by the tobacco growers and I dutifully pointed out their contribution to the economy. I particularly admired some of their techniques to beat the climate. These included irrigated nurseries and planting out before the rains with 1 litre of water per plant. Dr. Timothy Stamps, Zimbabwe's Welsh-born Minister of Health, once wickedly suggested the country should export 100% of tobacco instead of 99%!

Harare was chosen as the site of a major Conference on Tobacco and Health in 1993.[13] Theresa and I were invited to present a joint paper on "National Dependence on Tobacco – A case study". By the time the Conference took place we were in Zambia at St. Francis Hospital, Katete, near to Malawi – another tobacco dependent country. I was given a ticket to go back and present the paper. Theresa's part of the paper concentrated on the effects of tobacco on the health of Zimbabweans while I looked more at what alternative crops were available. A promising one was paprika but it did not have sufficient potential for employment or income. The World Health Organisation's campaign against tobacco has gone along extraordinarily well – but mainly in western countries. Africa remains a huge challenge and steps need to be taken to head off targeting for higher consumption in Africa.

A problem for those of us in the west, who are concerned about Africa, is that we are not geared to waiting for situations to develop. In talking to professional Zimbabweans on our last visit many seemed prepared to wait for the government to implode. Although clearly very unhappy with what was happening they did not have much hope that the Movement for Multi-Party Democracy (MMD) would be able to take over. When one looks at the history of Europe it is interesting that the "Dark Ages" lasted from the fall of the Roman Empire – around AD 475 – until the revival of learning – around AD 1137. We should be a bit more patient and not condemn African countries immediately "things fall apart" – to use the title of the famous Nigerian novel.

A key to Africa's recovery is that we in the west must find ways of building trust. The attempt by some politicians to boycott Zimbabwe has not helped the situation. "Less militant righteousness" is needed as in the Sudan.

One of the most impressive and hopeful developments, although fraught with setbacks, is the way some African countries have developed into nations over the past 50 years. Tribal loyalties are still to be found, as they are in Britain or in Europe, but the national loyalty is foremost in the countries that come to mind. They include, in particular, Tanzania, Botswana and Zambia but doubtless there are several others. Obviously Botswana has the advantage of a common African language but Tanzania has built its national spirit on Ki-Swahili and Zambia on English.

A visit to Harare's Heroes Acre we made in 1997 with a friend from Epworth gave an interesting insight into dashed hopes for a more even handed future for Southern Africa. In a House of Lords debate[14] in 1953 the Archbishop of Canterbury hoped "the proportionate place held by Europeans will steadily diminish and the place occupied by Africans will steadily increase as the results of economic development and educational and social development have their effect". Balanced development in Zimbabwe seemed to be happening when we lived in Zimbabwe from 1990-93 but perhaps it wasn't balanced enough. A letter from B. Ndlovu of Mkoba in the *Zimbabwe Independent* of 3/9/99 claimed Zimbabweans had become poorer since 1980. He describes "the plundering of national wealth by ministers, government officials and political chefs" and the diverting of funds from the communal lands to the farms of party leaders. I am confident that Zimbabwe will recover from its current period of misrule.

Some of those commemorated in Heroes Acre could have had a positive influence. I think in particular of Guy Clutton-Brock (1906-1995), Herbert Chitepo (1923-1975) and Josiah Tongogara (died "in a car accident in Mozambique on December 26 1979)". The challenge in South Africa is to ensure that the hopes for economic and social development are realized and not squandered as in Zimbabwe.

Guy Clutton-Brock we knew from 1959 when he and his wife Molly stayed with us in Bechuanaland after his detention in Southern Rhodesia. While delivering footballs and education materials in 1978-9 on behalf of British Quakers I met Josiah Chinamano (1923-1984). My contact in the ZIPRA depot in Lusaka was Edward Ndlovu (1926-1989) who welcomed me when I went to Parliament in Harare in 1982 on the invitation of the Speaker, Didymus Mutasa. Edward was a deputy minister when he died and had been appointed "following the unity accord between ZANU and ZAPU which he helped forge".[15] Disunity in political circles is at the heart of Zimbabwe's problems. This is not just a question of the Fifth Brigade suppression in Matabeleland and the Midlands during 1983-87. The questions that need answering are:-

1. Were Robert Mugabe's speeches on reconciliation, such as the one to the OAU Assembly on 2 July 1980, the result of a change of attitude or purely strategic ploys to delay a collapse in the economy?

2. Did Zimbabwean whites respond sufficiently to the reconciliation moves to ensure that they would have a continuing role?

When I spoke to several branches of the Commercial Farmers Union (CFU) in 1992-3 on "land reform in Kenya and Zambia" I had no feeling that they saw that some acceleration of land reform was essential for their survival.

In other words I did not get the impression that "the reality of the 'new situation' has been accepted by those who fought each other so bitterly".[16]

In retrospect we should have foreseen the disastrous Zimbabwe land policy. Soon after our arrival in Harare we attended the tenth anniversary of independence on April 18th 1990 in the National Sports Stadium. A banner proclaimed: "LAND TO THE PEOPLE BY THE YEAR 2000". We arrived at 8.30 as requested on the ticket to find the stadium almost empty. At the time we left in the afternoon it was full and we witnessed a stampede at a gate which ended with a mound of people being trampled. Fortunately there were no deaths. Joshua Nkomo had still not been fully re-integrated in the Government but his photo on the huge screen was the only one to be cheered. Guests included Nelson Mandela who was at the end of his first African tour after his release from prison. Next day I was on the same flight with him to Johannesburg and for a few minutes he sat in the tourist section to talk to some of his party. I probably broke the law by taking a photo (without flash) of the back of his head! It was an exhilarating time in South Africa and I hung around the airport to see him being welcomed home. Mandela's contribution to the future of both South Africa and the whole of the continent has been immense.

In a Radio 4 'Choice' interview on 7th December 2004 Morgan Tzvingirai claimed that the pivotal period for the decline of

171

Zimbabwe's economy was when the War Veterans demanded 4 billion Zim dollars towards gratuities and monthly pensions to 50,000 war veterans. The invasion of white farms followed and devaluation of the currency meant the pensions became worthless. The refusal at the Lancaster House Conference in 1979 by Britain to buy out white farmers as was done in Kenya contributed to this situation.

There is a reasonable prospect that enough commercial farmers and companies will survive to rebuild the large-scale sector. In the 21st century all African countries will need a large-scale farming sector in particular for crops that are best grown on a large-scale such as irrigated sugar, wheat, soya beans and barley. Dairy farms in Zimbabwe obtained special treatment.[17] It has been so long since Zimbabwe had some favourable reporting that it may be forgotten that Robert Mugabe's government developed one of the best family planning programmes in the 1980's. According to "The Greening of Africa"[18] its name was changed to emphasise child spacing and it was directed by a Ghanian, Dr. Boohene, Mugabe's sister-in-law. Techniques included oral contraceptives but it is worth pointing out that the condom serves both as a contraceptive and the main protection against HIV. Hopefully the use of condoms will help to ensure that fewer children are conceived accidentally.

In concluding this chapter it is worth remembering that several African economies performed well immediately after independence. I can remember, for instance, Kenneth Kaunda's Zambia being held up as an example to the rest of Africa in the post independence period from the mid 1960's to the mid 1970's. The collapse of the economy was the result of the world oil crisis, drastic falls in the price of copper and Ian Smith's UDI. When we arrived in 1977 it was clear that civil servants had got used to spending quite lavishly. A failure to adjust government spending to balance with tax revenue was a cause of both the debt crisis and the devaluation of currencies. Hopefully lessons have been learnt and the twenty first century will see greater realism.

Some readers will be surprised to see Zimbabwe mentioned in relation to hopes for the future in Africa. We worked there from 1990-93 and visited in 1994, 1997, 2000 and 2002. From 1959-61 and 1980-87 we visited regularly from Botswana and Zambia. During 1999-2002 the economy had almost collapsed but much of the country continued to function with amazing resilience. In 2002 we went as tourists on the Bulawayo-Harare express coach to a game ranch in the Midlands. There was no hostility to us as being from Britain and it appears that much of the government anti-British propaganda has had little impact. When the Mugabe regime is voted out or collapses, as it must, I am confident that the country will re-establish itself as one of Africa's success stories. In many ways Zimbabwe is an example of whether Tony Blair's vision of the rest of the world working with Africa can overcome setbacks.

The suggestion of former President Clinton that Tsunami aid should be supplied through twinning donor countries and those countries affected by the disaster has obvious advantages for a programme where speed of response is crucial. But it would also make sense in the case of long-term aid to Africa. In the 1960's, 70's and 80's much aid was dissipated through Cold War rivalries. While in the Gambia we tried to follow up some contacts we had made on our Welsh farm in 2002. We had been invited to meet a group from the village of Gunjur who are linked to the town of Marlborough in Wiltshire. The UK has a national organisation[19] for promoting links with communities in the South. The growth of tourism in African countries is, on balance, to be welcomed. It can help the rich of the west, and increasingly from the east, to be aware of the problems and needs of Africa.

Bob Geldof is confident that Africa's problems are solvable if western nations pull together. He will need to keep plugging away with his campaign for the rest of his lifetime.

If the Commission for Africa is to succeed all, or at least most of the following issues need to be considered:-

1. A ban on arms exports to African countries by all participants, but carefully controlled support to peace-keeping initiatives.

2. Aid to be channeled through ngo's or specific government departments such as health, agriculture and education as it was prior to independence in some countries.[20]

3. While subsidies like the CAP should be phased out in Europe and the USA, African countries should be allowed limited subsidies for emerging industries.

4. All tariffs on goods imported from Africa should be removed but African countries should be allowed to tariff imports from

western countries where unfair competition is proven. A particular case is second hand clothing which can undermine African textile industries but is of great benefit to poorer people.

5. All EU countries should legislate to ensure labelling of goods with the country of origin and campaigns should be started to favour imports from Africa.

6. Emphasis should be placed on providing a comprehensive health service covering such essentials as sexually transmitted diseases, and contraception as well as TB, HIV, malaria treatments and preventive measures. Funds should be channelled through ngo's wherever they exist, as well as governments.

7. Funding for education should emphasise practical and business skills, while the proportion devoted to PhD studies could be reduced.

8. An enquiry to follow-up ex-President Clinton's suggestion that different countries should be twinned with Western countries so that more comprehensive, long-term aid programmes can be developed. The former colonial powers could then be relieved of prime responsibility for certain countries.

9. A major effort should be made with tax and other incentives to encourage British importers to develop processing and packaging in African countries e.g. Cocoa, Coffee, Tea, Spices, Nuts and Sugar products.

10. African countries could be encouraged to follow the Malawi example and offer 'permanent residence' status to retired expatriate doctors, agriculturalists and others.

11. Major attention should be given to water supplies and sanitation with a view to: a) reducing the use of flush toilets; b) utilising more compost toilets; c) ensuring long-term maintenance of piped and/or pumped supplies; d) rainwater collection and storage; and e) recycling of sewage water and solids.

12. Water should also feature in aid to agriculture because of the great need to increase Africa's capacity to irrigate. Aid to the Nile Valley countries should be accelerated. Huge reductions of evaporation losses are possible in the Sudan if the swamps of the Upper Nile province were developed. If this was done by international agreement water from the White and Blue

Nile rivers could be allocated for irrigation to Ethiopia and East Africa.

NOTES

1. A slogan produced by the World Health Organisation in the 1980's.
2. Empire by Niall Ferguson. Allen Lane, The Penguin Press, 2003, London.
3. Obituary of Sir Paul Foot, (1916-2004) in Daily Telegraph : 8th April 2004.
4. Daily Telegraph 11/10/04.
5. Faith in Development. Edited by Deryke Belshaw et al. Regnum International, P.O. Box 70, OXFORD 0X2 6HB.
6. Surprised by Laughter by Stephen Carr. The Memoir Club, Stanhope Old Hall, Weardale, Co. Durham, UK.
7. Summary of Conference on Agriculture and Food Security in Eastern Africa. 1998, Limuru, Kenya.
8. Merfyn Temple. "New Hope for Africa", Taurus Publishing, Reading, Berkshire, 1991.
9. J.H. Oldham, New Hope in Africa, Longmans, London 1955.
10. Richard Hughes, Capricorn. The Radcliffe Press, 321 pp. London W2 4BV.
11. Basil Davidson. Modern Africa. Longman Harlow CM20 2JE, U.K. 1983.
12. S.A. Okuonzi, M.D. Dying for Economic Growth? Evidence of a flawed policy in Uganda. *The Lancet* Vol 364, October 30 2004, page 1632.
13. Proceedings of the All African Conference on Tobacco and Health. 14-17 November 1993, Harare, Zimbabwe. Edited by D Yach and S Harrison.
14. Hansard. 2 April 1953, Col. 602.
15. Government Printer. A Guide to the Heroes Acre. 1998, Harare.
16. Quote from Page 133. Victor de Waal. The Politics of Reconciliation, Hurst & Co., London, 1990.
17. Ernest Mapunga, chairperson of the Zimbabwe Dairy Industry, revealed in the South African Farmer's Weekly (29/1/05)how many dairy farms were spared from the farm invasions.
18. Paul Harrison. The Greening of Africa. Paladin Grafton Books, London, 1987, pages 250-7.
19. UKOWLA. The Dutch Barn, Manton, SN8 1PS, U.K. www.ukowla.org.uk.
20. According to the 1959 Colonial Office Report on the Colony and Protectorate of Kenya (HMSO. London. 1960) an annual part of the net revenue came as "assistance from U.K. Government".

Fifty Years Working and Travelling in Africa

THERESA AND RONALD WATTS

1954   R – Sailed from Liverpool to Lagos, Nigeria – Rural Education Officer, Ibadan.

1955   R – Holiday by pick-up and hitch-hiking to Bamenda, Cameroon.

1956-67 T – Did pre-registration at Mulago Hospital Uganda and travelled in Tanganyika.

1957   R – Christmas with Birminghams at Legon University, Ghana and rail to Tafo.

1958   R – Sailed from Lagos to Pointe Noire, train to Brazzaville. Ferry to Leopoldville – Train to near Matadi. Collected by 4x4 to Maquela da Zomba (Angola). Train to Lake Tanganyika, Ferry to Kisoma. Train to Tabora and Mwanza. Steamer to Kisumu. Bus to Kampala. Train and bus to Mombasa. Sail to Zanzibar, Dar-es-Salaam and Beira. Train to Rusape, Salisbury, Bulawayo via Palapye to Johannesburg and Durban. Sail to Port Elizabeth. Car to Cape Town. Sail to UK on Dutch cargo boat.

1959   R – Completed Diploma in Agric. Econ. Oxford University. Married. Sailed with Theresa from Southampton to Cape Town. Bought VW and drove to Maseru and Serowe via Imperial Reserve, Mafeking.

1960   R – Drove Serowe to Kampala via Mozambique, Nyasaland, Northern Rhodesia, Tanganyika, and Kenya (Kaimosi) T and Marguerite – Air to UK.

1962   R & T Flew to Kampala and drove VW to Kaimosi, Kenya. Theresa – Friends Hospital. Ronald – KTTC.

1962-65 R to Tanganyika (climbed Kilimanjaro) T – Monthly MAF FlightsS to clinics in Serengeti and Trans Mara.

1965-66 R & T to Embu, Eastern Province, Kenya, R – Principal of Inst. of Agric. T – Med. Officer, Embu Hospital.

1966-72 Moved plus children from Embu to Makerere University, Kampala, Uganda. Horses by train. T – Mulago Hospital (TB) and Lecturer – Com. Med. R-Lecturer (UNICEF funded in Ag. Extension.

1972   Train and boat Kampala – Mombasa – Dar– Durban – Cape Town – Tenerife (Canary Islands) – London – Wales (Whole Family).

1973   R – International Coffee Organisation consultancy: Angola and S.W. Africa. Train to Salazar. Car to Oshakati, etc.

1974   R – OXFAM consultancy. Zaire (Kikwit, etc by MAF planes).

1975   R – FAO Rome consultancy – Young Farmers of Uganda. Geneva– to assist WCC with production of guidelines for Churches in Rural Development. Consultancy Sokoto, N. Nigeria. Car to Ibadan and Jos.

1977-86 R & T – Flew to Lusaka, Zambia to work for government in agricultural training, extension and TV programme. Theresa to University Teaching Hospital. Train on Tazara to Dar and Victoria Falls for holidays.

1987   R – Flew to Lusaka – Video for Harvest Help on Lake Kariba.

        T – Flew to Lusaka – consultant on water aid. Dutch company.

1988   R – Johannesburg for lecture tour and Botswana (C and SAYM – Quakers).

        – Khartoum and Geneina, Sudan (QPS refugee project).

1989	R – Rome, Douala and road to Bamenda, Cameroon (IFAD).
	Return via Abidjan, Ivory Coast(African Development Bank).
1990-93	T to Medical School, Harare. R to Durban to collect car.
	R – Flew to Windhoek and Swakopmund.- Conf. on Land Reform.
1992	T to Addis Ababa, Ethiopia for medical conference.
1993	T & R to London by air. R to Harare by air then car to Katete, Zambia via Zimbabwe, Mozambique and Malawi. T – St Francis Hospital (TB), Katete.
1994-95	Many visits by car to Malawi plus C & SAYM Port Elizabeth.
1995	T flew to Nairobi then road to Moi University, Eldoret.
	R drove through Malawi and Tanzania to Nairobi and Eldoret.
1996	R – Visit Kampala, Uganda with express coach from Eldoret.
	R & T – Car to Mombasa. Coastal ship to Dar-es-Salaam and Durban. T – Ngwelezane Hosp. (TB).
1997	R & T – Car to Gaborone, Botswana for C & SAYM (Quakers).
1998	R & T – Car to Swaziland, Harare, Marondera and Mazvingo.
1999	R & T – Italian cruise ship Durban – Reunion – Mauritius – Seychelles – Port Said and Genoa, Italy.
2000	R & T – Flew London to Nairobi, then Coach to Moshi (T teaching KCMC).
2001	R & T – Flew Air Namibia to Windhoek, Johannesburg and car to Botswana.
2002	R & T – Flew to Johannesburg and Bulawayo. T – flew to Nairobi to teach at TICH, Kisumu.
2003	R & T Flew to Johannesburg then car to Maseru (Lesotho).
	Also flew Bulawayo then coach to Kwe-Kwe and Sebakwe Conservancy

2004   R & T – Flew to Nairobi and Kisumu. Teaching at TICH. Land Rover to Poroko and Masai Mara. Hired Car to Eldoret (Keino Children's Home). Visit Kaimosi and Goibei.

R & T – Flew Bristol to Banjul, The Gambia for holiday and visits to MRC and NARI.

APPENDIX B

Acronyms

OXFAM	Oxford Committee for Famine Relief
MAF	Missionary Aviation Fellowship
FAO	Food and Agriculture Organisation
QPS	Quaker Peace and Service
IFAD	International Fund for Agricultural Development
C & SAYM	Central and Southern Africa Yearly Meeting (Quakers)
KCMC	Kilimanjaro Christian Medical College
TICH	Tropical Institute of Community Health
KTTC	Kaimosi Teacher Training College
WCC	World Council of Churches
BYM	Britain Yearly Meeting
IPPNW	International Physicians for the Prevention of Nuclear War
FOR	Fellowship of Reconciliation
CRFEA	Christian Rural Fellowship of East Africa
FSC	Friends Service Council
MRC	Medical Research Council
NARI	National Agricultural Research Institute
SCM	Student Christian Movement
WACRI	West African Cocoa Research Institute
UNICEF	United Nations Children's Emergency Fund

Index

IPPNW ix
Iran (Persia) 36
Iraq 36-37
Iron Curtain Aid & Visits
130-132

Jabavu, Noni 25, 33, 121
Jepson, Trevor viii, 125
Jews 34, 39
Joking Relationships 106, 113
Jolly, Dr Richard 147
Jones, Judge Jeffrey 91
Journalism 63

Kabaka 2
Kahn, Sam 33, 115
Kaimosi vii, 17, 22, 88, 103, 148
Kariba, Lake 27
Kaunda, Kenneth 12, 108, 111,
   114, 144, 172
Kenya 15, 17, 88-89, 122, 148
Kenyatta, Jomo 22
Khama, Seretse vii, 14, 17
Khama, Tshekedi vii, 14
Kiano, Julius 54
Kibaki, Mwai 22, 52
Kinoti, George 32, 137
Kruger Family 15, 18

Lancaster House 13
Land Reform 13, 18
Languages 24, 41, 79, 82, 103,
   170
Law 90-1
Leakey Family 58, 130
Leasehold Land 13
Lesotho 167, 179
Lessing, Doris 100
Leys, Colin 11
Liberal Party of S. Africa 17
Lighter Look Column 101, 106
Livingstone, D 7, 61
Loans & Credit 142, 143
London Hospital 1

Long-term Heads of Africa 161,
   174
Lutheran World Federation 32

Maesyreglwys Farm ix, 12, 82,
   164
Malawi (formerly Myasaland)
   11, 158
Makerere University vii, 31,
   51-2
Marketing 69, 143, 155
Marshall, Kageha (née Watts)
   vii, 88, 106, 107, 118
Martin, Walter viii, 122, 125
Mazrui, Ali 159
Mbithi, Philip 51
McCall, Smith, A 8
Mediation team of Quakers 125
Merwe, Hendrik Vander viii,
   129-30
Migratory Labour 33
Missionaries 4, 30, 37
Missing Americans Case 91
Mogoba, Stanley 115
Moi University viii, 15, 42
Moore, Stanley & Margaret 135
Mugabe, Robert 6, 122, 139,
   165
Multi-lingual Societies 82
Muslims & AIDS 37
Mutasa, Didymus 14, 125

Nabwera, Barudi 41, 50
Namibia 178-9
Nationalisation of Banks 90
Nationalisation of Canal 18
Ndegwa, Philip 143
Ndungane, Archbishop 24
NEPAD 7, 134, 167
Ngu, Victor x, 2, 80
Nigeria 9, 40-44
Nigerian Quakers 80
Nile Valley aid to Irrigation 96,
   175

182